Comparative Law: A Very Short Introduction

T0016924

Very Short Introductions available now:

ABOLITIONISM Richard S. Newman
THE ABRAHAMIC RELIGIONS
   Charles L. Cohen
ACCOUNTING Christopher Nobes
ADDICTION Keith Humphreys
ADOLESCENCE Peter K. Smith
THEODOR W. ADORNO
   Andrew Bowie
ADVERTISING Winston Fletcher
AERIAL WARFARE Frank Ledwidge
AESTHETICS Bence Nanay
AFRICAN AMERICAN HISTORY
   Jonathan Scott Holloway
AFRICAN AMERICAN RELIGION
   Eddie S. Glaude Jr.
AFRICAN HISTORY John Parker and
   Richard Rathbone
AFRICAN POLITICS Ian Taylor
AFRICAN RELIGIONS
   Jacob K. Olupona
AGEING Nancy A. Pachana
AGNOSTICISM Robin Le Poidevin
AGRICULTURE Paul Brassley and
   Richard Soffe
ALEXANDER THE GREAT
   Hugh Bowden
ALGEBRA Peter M. Higgins
AMERICAN BUSINESS HISTORY
   Walter A. Friedman
AMERICAN CULTURAL HISTORY
   Eric Avila
AMERICAN FOREIGN RELATIONS
   Andrew Preston
AMERICAN HISTORY Paul S. Boyer

AMERICAN IMMIGRATION
   David A. Gerber
AMERICAN INTELLECTUAL
   HISTORY
   Jennifer Ratner-Rosenhagen
THE AMERICAN JUDICIAL SYSTEM
   Charles L. Zelden
AMERICAN LEGAL HISTORY
   G. Edward White
AMERICAN MILITARY HISTORY
   Joseph T. Glatthaar
AMERICAN NAVAL HISTORY
   Craig L. Symonds
AMERICAN POETRY David Caplan
AMERICAN POLITICAL HISTORY
   Donald Critchlow
AMERICAN POLITICAL PARTIES
   AND ELECTIONS L. Sandy Maisel
AMERICAN POLITICS
   Richard M. Valelly
THE AMERICAN PRESIDENCY
   Charles O. Jones
THE AMERICAN REVOLUTION
   Robert J. Allison
AMERICAN SLAVERY
   Heather Andrea Williams
THE AMERICAN SOUTH
   Charles Reagan Wilson
THE AMERICAN WEST
   Stephen Aron
AMERICAN WOMEN'S HISTORY
   Susan Ware
AMPHIBIANS T. S. Kemp
ANAESTHESIA Aidan O'Donnell

ANALYTIC PHILOSOPHY
    Michael Beaney
ANARCHISM Alex Prichard
ANCIENT ASSYRIA Karen Radner
ANCIENT EGYPT Ian Shaw
ANCIENT EGYPTIAN ART AND
    ARCHITECTURE Christina Riggs
ANCIENT GREECE Paul Cartledge
ANCIENT GREEK AND ROMAN
    SCIENCE Liba Taub
THE ANCIENT NEAR EAST
    Amanda H. Podany
ANCIENT PHILOSOPHY Julia Annas
ANCIENT WARFARE
    Harry Sidebottom
ANGELS David Albert Jones
ANGLICANISM Mark Chapman
THE ANGLO-SAXON AGE John Blair
ANIMAL BEHAVIOUR
    Tristram D. Wyatt
THE ANIMAL KINGDOM
    Peter Holland
ANIMAL RIGHTS David DeGrazia
ANSELM Thomas Williams
THE ANTARCTIC Klaus Dodds
ANTHROPOCENE Erle C. Ellis
ANTISEMITISM Steven Beller
ANXIETY Daniel Freeman and
    Jason Freeman
THE APOCRYPHAL GOSPELS
    Paul Foster
APPLIED MATHEMATICS
    Alain Goriely
THOMAS AQUINAS Fergus Kerr
ARBITRATION Thomas Schultz and
    Thomas Grant
ARCHAEOLOGY Paul Bahn
ARCHITECTURE Andrew Ballantyne
THE ARCTIC Klaus Dodds and
    Jamie Woodward
HANNAH ARENDT Dana Villa
ARISTOCRACY William Doyle
ARISTOTLE Jonathan Barnes
ART HISTORY Dana Arnold
ART THEORY Cynthia Freeland
ARTIFICIAL INTELLIGENCE
    Margaret A. Boden
ASIAN AMERICAN HISTORY
    Madeline Y. Hsu
ASTROBIOLOGY David C. Catling

ASTROPHYSICS James Binney
ATHEISM Julian Baggini
THE ATMOSPHERE Paul I. Palmer
AUGUSTINE Henry Chadwick
JANE AUSTEN Tom Keymer
AUSTRALIA Kenneth Morgan
AUTISM Uta Frith
AUTOBIOGRAPHY Laura Marcus
THE AVANT GARDE David Cottington
THE AZTECS David Carrasco
BABYLONIA Trevor Bryce
BACTERIA Sebastian G. B. Amyes
BANKING John Goddard and
    John O. S. Wilson
BARTHES Jonathan Culler
THE BEATS David Sterritt
BEAUTY Roger Scruton
LUDWIG VAN BEETHOVEN
    Mark Evan Bonds
BEHAVIOURAL ECONOMICS
    Michelle Baddeley
BESTSELLERS John Sutherland
THE BIBLE John Riches
BIBLICAL ARCHAEOLOGY
    Eric H. Cline
BIG DATA Dawn E. Holmes
BIOCHEMISTRY Mark Lorch
BIODIVERSITY CONSERVATION
    David Macdonald
BIOGEOGRAPHY Mark V. Lomolino
BIOGRAPHY Hermione Lee
BIOMETRICS Michael Fairhurst
ELIZABETH BISHOP
    Jonathan F. S. Post
BLACK HOLES Katherine Blundell
BLASPHEMY Yvonne Sherwood
BLOOD Chris Cooper
THE BLUES Elijah Wald
THE BODY Chris Shilling
THE BOHEMIANS David Weir
NIELS BOHR J. L. Heilbron
THE BOOK OF COMMON PRAYER
    Brian Cummings
THE BOOK OF MORMON
    Terryl Givens
BORDERS Alexander C. Diener and
    Joshua Hagen
THE BRAIN Michael O'Shea
BRANDING Robert Jones
THE BRICS Andrew F. Cooper

BRITISH CINEMA Charles Barr
THE BRITISH CONSTITUTION
    Martin Loughlin
THE BRITISH EMPIRE Ashley Jackson
BRITISH POLITICS Tony Wright
BUDDHA Michael Carrithers
BUDDHISM Damien Keown
BUDDHIST ETHICS Damien Keown
BYZANTIUM Peter Sarris
CALVINISM Jon Balserak
ALBERT CAMUS Oliver Gloag
CANADA Donald Wright
CANCER Nicholas James
CAPITALISM James Fulcher
CATHOLICISM Gerald O'Collins
CAUSATION Stephen Mumford and
    Rani Lill Anjum
THE CELL Terence Allen and
    Graham Cowling
THE CELTS Barry Cunliffe
CHAOS Leonard Smith
GEOFFREY CHAUCER David Wallace
CHEMISTRY Peter Atkins
CHILD PSYCHOLOGY Usha Goswami
CHILDREN'S LITERATURE
    Kimberley Reynolds
CHINESE LITERATURE Sabina Knight
CHOICE THEORY Michael Allingham
CHRISTIAN ART Beth Williamson
CHRISTIAN ETHICS D. Stephen Long
CHRISTIANITY Linda Woodhead
CIRCADIAN RHYTHMS Russell Foster
    and Leon Kreitzman
CITIZENSHIP Richard Bellamy
CITY PLANNING Carl Abbott
CIVIL ENGINEERING
    David Muir Wood
THE CIVIL RIGHTS MOVEMENT
    Thomas C. Holt
CLASSICAL LITERATURE William Allan
CLASSICAL MYTHOLOGY
    Helen Morales
CLASSICS Mary Beard and
    John Henderson
CLAUSEWITZ Michael Howard
CLIMATE Mark Maslin
CLIMATE CHANGE Mark Maslin
CLINICAL PSYCHOLOGY
    Susan Llewelyn and
    Katie Aafjes-van Doorn

COGNITIVE BEHAVIOURAL
    THERAPY Freda McManus
COGNITIVE NEUROSCIENCE
    Richard Passingham
THE COLD WAR Robert J. McMahon
COLONIAL AMERICA Alan Taylor
COLONIAL LATIN AMERICAN
    LITERATURE Rolena Adorno
COMBINATORICS Robin Wilson
COMEDY Matthew Bevis
COMMUNISM Leslie Holmes
COMPARATIVE LAW Sabrina Ragone
    and Guido Smorto
COMPARATIVE LITERATURE
    Ben Hutchinson
COMPETITION AND ANTITRUST
    LAW Ariel Ezrachi
COMPLEXITY John H. Holland
THE COMPUTER Darrel Ince
COMPUTER SCIENCE
    Subrata Dasgupta
CONCENTRATION CAMPS
    Dan Stone
CONDENSED MATTER
    PHYSICS Ross H. McKenzie
CONFUCIANISM Daniel K. Gardner
THE CONQUISTADORS
    Matthew Restall and
    Felipe Fernández-Armesto
CONSCIENCE Paul Strohm
CONSCIOUSNESS Susan Blackmore
CONTEMPORARY ART
    Julian Stallabrass
CONTEMPORARY FICTION
    Robert Eaglestone
CONTINENTAL PHILOSOPHY
    Simon Critchley
COPERNICUS Owen Gingerich
CORAL REEFS Charles Sheppard
CORPORATE SOCIAL
    RESPONSIBILITY Jeremy Moon
CORRUPTION Leslie Holmes
COSMOLOGY Peter Coles
COUNTRY MUSIC Richard Carlin
CREATIVITY Vlad Glăveanu
CRIME FICTION Richard Bradford
CRIMINAL JUSTICE Julian V. Roberts
CRIMINOLOGY Tim Newburn
CRITICAL THEORY
    Stephen Eric Bronner

THE CRUSADES Christopher Tyerman
CRYPTOGRAPHY Fred Piper and
    Sean Murphy
CRYSTALLOGRAPHY A. M. Glazer
THE CULTURAL REVOLUTION
    Richard Curt Kraus
DADA AND SURREALISM
    David Hopkins
DANTE Peter Hainsworth and
    David Robey
DARWIN Jonathan Howard
THE DEAD SEA SCROLLS
    Timothy H. Lim
DECADENCE David Weir
DECOLONIZATION Dane Kennedy
DEMENTIA Kathleen Taylor
DEMOCRACY Naomi Zack
DEMOGRAPHY Sarah Harper
DEPRESSION Jan Scott and
    Mary Jane Tacchi
DERRIDA Simon Glendinning
DESCARTES Tom Sorell
DESERTS Nick Middleton
DESIGN John Heskett
DEVELOPMENT Ian Goldin
DEVELOPMENTAL BIOLOGY
    Lewis Wolpert
THE DEVIL Darren Oldridge
DIASPORA Kevin Kenny
CHARLES DICKENS Jenny Hartley
DICTIONARIES Lynda Mugglestone
DINOSAURS David Norman
DIPLOMATIC HISTORY
    Joseph M. Siracusa
DOCUMENTARY FILM
    Patricia Aufderheide
DREAMING J. Allan Hobson
DRUGS Les Iversen
DRUIDS Barry Cunliffe
DYNASTY Jeroen Duindam
DYSLEXIA Margaret J. Snowling
EARLY MUSIC Thomas Forrest Kelly
THE EARTH Martin Redfern
EARTH SYSTEM SCIENCE Tim Lenton
ECOLOGY Jaboury Ghazoul
ECONOMICS Partha Dasgupta
EDUCATION Gary Thomas
EGYPTIAN MYTH Geraldine Pinch
EIGHTEENTH-CENTURY BRITAIN
    Paul Langford

THE ELEMENTS Philip Ball
EMOTION Dylan Evans
EMPIRE Stephen Howe
EMPLOYMENT LAW David Cabrelli
ENERGY SYSTEMS Nick Jenkins
ENGELS Terrell Carver
ENGINEERING David Blockley
THE ENGLISH LANGUAGE
    Simon Horobin
ENGLISH LITERATURE Jonathan Bate
THE ENLIGHTENMENT
    John Robertson
ENTREPRENEURSHIP Paul Westhead
    and Mike Wright
ENVIRONMENTAL ECONOMICS
    Stephen Smith
ENVIRONMENTAL ETHICS
    Robin Attfield
ENVIRONMENTAL LAW
    Elizabeth Fisher
ENVIRONMENTAL POLITICS
    Andrew Dobson
ENZYMES Paul Engel
EPICUREANISM Catherine Wilson
EPIDEMIOLOGY Rodolfo Saracci
ETHICS Simon Blackburn
ETHNOMUSICOLOGY Timothy Rice
THE ETRUSCANS Christopher Smith
EUGENICS Philippa Levine
THE EUROPEAN UNION
    Simon Usherwood and John Pinder
EUROPEAN UNION LAW
    Anthony Arnull
EVANGELICALISM
    John G. Stackhouse Jr.
EVIL Luke Russell
EVOLUTION Brian and
    Deborah Charlesworth
EXISTENTIALISM Thomas Flynn
EXPLORATION Stewart A. Weaver
EXTINCTION Paul B. Wignall
THE EYE Michael Land
FAIRY TALE Marina Warner
FAMILY LAW Jonathan Herring
MICHAEL FARADAY
    Frank A. J. L. James
FASCISM Kevin Passmore
FASHION Rebecca Arnold
FEDERALISM Mark J. Rozell and
    Clyde Wilcox

FEMINISM Margaret Walters
FILM Michael Wood
FILM MUSIC Kathryn Kalinak
FILM NOIR James Naremore
FIRE Andrew C. Scott
THE FIRST WORLD WAR
    Michael Howard
FLUID MECHANICS Eric Lauga
FOLK MUSIC Mark Slobin
FOOD John Krebs
FORENSIC PSYCHOLOGY
    David Canter
FORENSIC SCIENCE Jim Fraser
FORESTS Jaboury Ghazoul
FOSSILS Keith Thomson
FOUCAULT Gary Gutting
THE FOUNDING FATHERS
    R. B. Bernstein
FRACTALS Kenneth Falconer
FREE SPEECH Nigel Warburton
FREE WILL Thomas Pink
FREEMASONRY Andreas Önnerfors
FRENCH CINEMA Dudley Andrew
FRENCH LITERATURE John D. Lyons
FRENCH PHILOSOPHY
    Stephen Gaukroger and Knox Peden
THE FRENCH REVOLUTION
    William Doyle
FREUD Anthony Storr
FUNDAMENTALISM Malise Ruthven
FUNGI Nicholas P. Money
THE FUTURE Jennifer M. Gidley
GALAXIES John Gribbin
GALILEO Stillman Drake
GAME THEORY Ken Binmore
GANDHI Bhikhu Parekh
GARDEN HISTORY Gordon Campbell
GENES Jonathan Slack
GENIUS Andrew Robinson
GENOMICS John Archibald
GEOGRAPHY John Matthews and
    David Herbert
GEOLOGY Jan Zalasiewicz
GEOMETRY Maciej Dunajski
GEOPHYSICS William Lowrie
GEOPOLITICS Klaus Dodds
GERMAN LITERATURE Nicholas Boyle
GERMAN PHILOSOPHY
    Andrew Bowie
THE GHETTO Bryan Cheyette
GLACIATION David J. A. Evans
GLOBAL CATASTROPHES Bill McGuire
GLOBAL ECONOMIC HISTORY
    Robert C. Allen
GLOBAL ISLAM Nile Green
GLOBALIZATION Manfred B. Steger
GOD John Bowker
GÖDEL'S THEOREM A. W. Moore
GOETHE Ritchie Robertson
THE GOTHIC Nick Groom
GOVERNANCE Mark Bevir
GRAVITY Timothy Clifton
THE GREAT DEPRESSION AND
    THE NEW DEAL Eric Rauchway
HABEAS CORPUS Amanda L. Tyler
HABERMAS James Gordon Finlayson
THE HABSBURG EMPIRE
    Martyn Rady
HAPPINESS Daniel M. Haybron
THE HARLEM RENAISSANCE
    Cheryl A. Wall
THE HEBREW BIBLE AS LITERATURE
    Tod Linafelt
HEGEL Peter Singer
HEIDEGGER Michael Inwood
THE HELLENISTIC AGE
    Peter Thonemann
HEREDITY John Waller
HERMENEUTICS Jens Zimmermann
HERODOTUS Jennifer T. Roberts
HIEROGLYPHS Penelope Wilson
HINDUISM Kim Knott
HISTORY John H. Arnold
THE HISTORY OF ASTRONOMY
    Michael Hoskin
THE HISTORY OF CHEMISTRY
    William H. Brock
THE HISTORY OF CHILDHOOD
    James Marten
THE HISTORY OF CINEMA
    Geoffrey Nowell-Smith
THE HISTORY OF COMPUTING
    Doron Swade
THE HISTORY OF EMOTIONS
    Thomas Dixon
THE HISTORY OF LIFE Michael Benton
THE HISTORY OF MATHEMATICS
    Jacqueline Stedall
THE HISTORY OF MEDICINE
    William Bynum

THE HISTORY OF PHYSICS
    J. L. Heilbron
THE HISTORY OF POLITICAL
    THOUGHT Richard Whatmore
THE HISTORY OF TIME
    Leofranc Holford-Strevens
HIV AND AIDS Alan Whiteside
HOBBES Richard Tuck
HOLLYWOOD Peter Decherney
THE HOLY ROMAN EMPIRE
    Joachim Whaley
HOME Michael Allen Fox
HOMER Barbara Graziosi
HORACE Llewelyn Morgan
HORMONES Martin Luck
HORROR Darryl Jones
HUMAN ANATOMY Leslie Klenerman
HUMAN EVOLUTION Bernard Wood
HUMAN PHYSIOLOGY
    Jamie A. Davies
HUMAN RESOURCE
    MANAGEMENT Adrian Wilkinson
HUMAN RIGHTS Andrew Clapham
HUMANISM Stephen Law
HUME James A. Harris
HUMOUR Noël Carroll
IBN SĪNĀ (AVICENNA)
    Peter Adamson
THE ICE AGE Jamie Woodward
IDENTITY Florian Coulmas
IDEOLOGY Michael Freeden
IMAGINATION
    Jennifer Gosetti-Ferencei
THE IMMUNE SYSTEM
    Paul Klenerman
INDIAN CINEMA Ashish Rajadhyaksha
INDIAN PHILOSOPHY Sue Hamilton
THE INDUSTRIAL REVOLUTION
    Robert C. Allen
INFECTIOUS DISEASE Marta L. Wayne
    and Benjamin M. Bolker
INFINITY Ian Stewart
INFORMATION Luciano Floridi
INNOVATION Mark Dodgson and
    David Gann
INTELLECTUAL PROPERTY
    Siva Vaidhyanathan
INTELLIGENCE Ian J. Deary
INTERNATIONAL LAW
    Vaughan Lowe
INTERNATIONAL MIGRATION
    Khalid Koser
INTERNATIONAL RELATIONS
    Christian Reus-Smit
INTERNATIONAL SECURITY
    Christopher S. Browning
INSECTS Simon Leather
INVASIVE SPECIES Julie Lockwood and
    Dustin Welbourne
IRAN Ali M. Ansari
ISLAM Malise Ruthven
ISLAMIC HISTORY Adam Silverstein
ISLAMIC LAW Mashood A. Baderin
ISOTOPES Rob Ellam
ITALIAN LITERATURE
    Peter Hainsworth and David Robey
HENRY JAMES Susan L. Mizruchi
JAPANESE LITERATURE Alan Tansman
JESUS Richard Bauckham
JEWISH HISTORY David N. Myers
JEWISH LITERATURE Ilan Stavans
JOURNALISM Ian Hargreaves
JAMES JOYCE Colin MacCabe
JUDAISM Norman Solomon
JUNG Anthony Stevens
THE JURY Renée Lettow Lerner
KABBALAH Joseph Dan
KAFKA Ritchie Robertson
KANT Roger Scruton
KEYNES Robert Skidelsky
KIERKEGAARD Patrick Gardiner
KNOWLEDGE Jennifer Nagel
THE KORAN Michael Cook
KOREA Michael J. Seth
LAKES Warwick F. Vincent
LANDSCAPE ARCHITECTURE
    Ian H. Thompson
LANDSCAPES AND
    GEOMORPHOLOGY
    Andrew Goudie and Heather Viles
LANGUAGES Stephen R. Anderson
LATE ANTIQUITY Gillian Clark
LAW Raymond Wacks
THE LAWS OF THERMODYNAMICS
    Peter Atkins
LEADERSHIP Keith Grint
LEARNING Mark Haselgrove
LEIBNIZ Maria Rosa Antognazza
C. S. LEWIS James Como
LIBERALISM Michael Freeden

LIGHT Ian Walmsley
LINCOLN Allen C. Guelzo
LINGUISTICS Peter Matthews
LITERARY THEORY Jonathan Culler
LOCKE John Dunn
LOGIC Graham Priest
LOVE Ronald de Sousa
MARTIN LUTHER Scott H. Hendrix
MACHIAVELLI Quentin Skinner
MADNESS Andrew Scull
MAGIC Owen Davies
MAGNA CARTA Nicholas Vincent
MAGNETISM Stephen Blundell
MALTHUS Donald Winch
MAMMALS T. S. Kemp
MANAGEMENT John Hendry
NELSON MANDELA Elleke Boehmer
MAO Delia Davin
MARINE BIOLOGY Philip V. Mladenov
MARKETING
    Kenneth Le Meunier-FitzHugh
THE MARQUIS DE SADE John Phillips
MARTYRDOM Jolyon Mitchell
MARX Peter Singer
MATERIALS Christopher Hall
MATHEMATICAL ANALYSIS
    Richard Earl
MATHEMATICAL FINANCE
    Mark H. A. Davis
MATHEMATICS Timothy Gowers
MATTER Geoff Cottrell
THE MAYA Matthew Restall and
    Amara Solari
THE MEANING OF LIFE
    Terry Eagleton
MEASUREMENT David Hand
MEDICAL ETHICS Michael Dunn and
    Tony Hope
MEDICAL LAW Charles Foster
MEDIEVAL BRITAIN John Gillingham
    and Ralph A. Griffiths
MEDIEVAL LITERATURE
    Elaine Treharne
MEDIEVAL PHILOSOPHY
    John Marenbon
MEMORY Jonathan K. Foster
METAPHYSICS Stephen Mumford
METHODISM William J. Abraham
THE MEXICAN REVOLUTION
    Alan Knight

MICROBIOLOGY Nicholas P. Money
MICROBIOMES Angela E. Douglas
MICROECONOMICS Avinash Dixit
MICROSCOPY Terence Allen
THE MIDDLE AGES Miri Rubin
MILITARY JUSTICE Eugene R. Fidell
MILITARY STRATEGY
    Antulio J. Echevarria II
JOHN STUART MILL Gregory Claeys
MINERALS David Vaughan
MIRACLES Yujin Nagasawa
MODERN ARCHITECTURE
    Adam Sharr
MODERN ART David Cottington
MODERN BRAZIL Anthony W. Pereira
MODERN CHINA Rana Mitter
MODERN DRAMA
    Kirsten E. Shepherd-Barr
MODERN FRANCE
    Vanessa R. Schwartz
MODERN INDIA Craig Jeffrey
MODERN IRELAND Senia Pašeta
MODERN ITALY Anna Cento Bull
MODERN JAPAN
    Christopher Goto-Jones
MODERN LATIN AMERICAN
    LITERATURE
    Roberto González Echevarría
MODERN WAR Richard English
MODERNISM Christopher Butler
MOLECULAR BIOLOGY Aysha Divan
    and Janice A. Royds
MOLECULES Philip Ball
MONASTICISM Stephen J. Davis
THE MONGOLS Morris Rossabi
MONTAIGNE William M. Hamlin
MOONS David A. Rothery
MORMONISM
    Richard Lyman Bushman
MOUNTAINS Martin F. Price
MUHAMMAD Jonathan A. C. Brown
MULTICULTURALISM Ali Rattansi
MULTILINGUALISM John C. Maher
MUSIC Nicholas Cook
MUSIC AND TECHNOLOGY
    Mark Katz
MYTH Robert A. Segal
NANOTECHNOLOGY
    Philip Moriarty
NAPOLEON David A. Bell

THE NAPOLEONIC WARS
  Mike Rapport
NATIONALISM Steven Grosby
NATIVE AMERICAN LITERATURE
  Sean Teuton
NAVIGATION Jim Bennett
NAZI GERMANY Jane Caplan
NEGOTIATION Carrie Menkel-Meadow
NEOLIBERALISM Manfred B. Steger
  and Ravi K. Roy
NETWORKS Guido Caldarelli and
  Michele Catanzaro
THE NEW TESTAMENT
  Luke Timothy Johnson
THE NEW TESTAMENT AS
  LITERATURE Kyle Keefer
NEWTON Robert Iliffe
NIETZSCHE Michael Tanner
NINETEENTH-CENTURY BRITAIN
  Christopher Harvie and
  H. C. G. Matthew
THE NORMAN CONQUEST
  George Garnett
NORTH AMERICAN INDIANS
  Theda Perdue and Michael D. Green
NORTHERN IRELAND
  Marc Mulholland
NOTHING Frank Close
NUCLEAR PHYSICS Frank Close
NUCLEAR POWER Maxwell Irvine
NUCLEAR WEAPONS
  Joseph M. Siracusa
NUMBER THEORY Robin Wilson
NUMBERS Peter M. Higgins
NUTRITION David A. Bender
OBJECTIVITY Stephen Gaukroger
OBSERVATIONAL ASTRONOMY
  Geoff Cottrell
OCEANS Dorrik Stow
THE OLD TESTAMENT
  Michael D. Coogan
THE ORCHESTRA D. Kern Holoman
ORGANIC CHEMISTRY
  Graham Patrick
ORGANIZATIONS Mary Jo Hatch
ORGANIZED CRIME
  Georgios A. Antonopoulos and
  Georgios Papanicolaou
ORTHODOX CHRISTIANITY
  A. Edward Siecienski
OVID Llewelyn Morgan
PAGANISM Owen Davies
PAKISTAN Pippa Virdee
THE PALESTINIAN-ISRAELI
  CONFLICT Martin Bunton
PANDEMICS Christian W. McMillen
PARTICLE PHYSICS Frank Close
PAUL E. P. Sanders
IVAN PAVLOV Daniel P. Todes
PEACE Oliver P. Richmond
PENTECOSTALISM William K. Kay
PERCEPTION Brian Rogers
THE PERIODIC TABLE Eric R. Scerri
PHILOSOPHICAL METHOD
  Timothy Williamson
PHILOSOPHY Edward Craig
PHILOSOPHY IN THE ISLAMIC
  WORLD Peter Adamson
PHILOSOPHY OF BIOLOGY
  Samir Okasha
PHILOSOPHY OF LAW
  Raymond Wacks
PHILOSOPHY OF MIND
  Barbara Gail Montero
PHILOSOPHY OF PHYSICS
  David Wallace
PHILOSOPHY OF SCIENCE
  Samir Okasha
PHILOSOPHY OF RELIGION
  Tim Bayne
PHOTOGRAPHY Steve Edwards
PHYSICAL CHEMISTRY Peter Atkins
PHYSICS Sidney Perkowitz
PILGRIMAGE Ian Reader
PLAGUE Paul Slack
PLANETARY SYSTEMS
  Raymond T. Pierrehumbert
PLANETS David A. Rothery
PLANTS Timothy Walker
PLATE TECTONICS Peter Molnar
PLATO Julia Annas
POETRY Bernard O'Donoghue
POLITICAL PHILOSOPHY
  David Miller
POLITICS Kenneth Minogue
POLYGAMY Sarah M. S. Pearsall
POPULISM Cas Mudde and
  Cristóbal Rovira Kaltwasser
POSTCOLONIALISM Robert J. C. Young
POSTMODERNISM Christopher Butler

POSTSTRUCTURALISM
    Catherine Belsey
POVERTY Philip N. Jefferson
PREHISTORY Chris Gosden
PRESOCRATIC PHILOSOPHY
    Catherine Osborne
PRIVACY Raymond Wacks
PROBABILITY John Haigh
PROGRESSIVISM Walter Nugent
PROHIBITION W. J. Rorabaugh
PROJECTS Andrew Davies
PROTESTANTISM Mark A. Noll
PSEUDOSCIENCE Michael D. Gordin
PSYCHIATRY Tom Burns
PSYCHOANALYSIS Daniel Pick
PSYCHOLOGY Gillian Butler and
    Freda McManus
PSYCHOLOGY OF MUSIC
    Elizabeth Hellmuth Margulis
PSYCHOPATHY Essi Viding
PSYCHOTHERAPY Tom Burns and
    Eva Burns-Lundgren
PUBLIC ADMINISTRATION
    Stella Z. Theodoulou and Ravi K. Roy
PUBLIC HEALTH Virginia Berridge
PURITANISM Francis J. Bremer
THE QUAKERS Pink Dandelion
QUANTUM THEORY
    John Polkinghorne
RACISM Ali Rattansi
RADIOACTIVITY Claudio Tuniz
RASTAFARI Ennis B. Edmonds
READING Belinda Jack
THE REAGAN REVOLUTION Gil Troy
REALITY Jan Westerhoff
RECONSTRUCTION Allen C. Guelzo
THE REFORMATION Peter Marshall
REFUGEES Gil Loescher
RELATIVITY Russell Stannard
RELIGION Thomas A. Tweed
RELIGION IN AMERICA Timothy Beal
THE RENAISSANCE Jerry Brotton
RENAISSANCE ART
    Geraldine A. Johnson
RENEWABLE ENERGY Nick Jelley
REPTILES T. S. Kemp
REVOLUTIONS Jack A. Goldstone
RHETORIC Richard Toye
RISK Baruch Fischhoff and John Kadvany
RITUAL Barry Stephenson

RIVERS Nick Middleton
ROBOTICS Alan Winfield
ROCKS Jan Zalasiewicz
ROMAN BRITAIN Peter Salway
THE ROMAN EMPIRE
    Christopher Kelly
THE ROMAN REPUBLIC
    David M. Gwynn
ROMANTICISM Michael Ferber
ROUSSEAU Robert Wokler
RUSSELL A. C. Grayling
THE RUSSIAN ECONOMY
    Richard Connolly
RUSSIAN HISTORY Geoffrey Hosking
RUSSIAN LITERATURE Catriona Kelly
THE RUSSIAN REVOLUTION
    S. A. Smith
SAINTS Simon Yarrow
SAMURAI Michael Wert
SAVANNAS Peter A. Furley
SCEPTICISM Duncan Pritchard
SCHIZOPHRENIA Chris Frith and
    Eve Johnstone
SCHOPENHAUER
    Christopher Janaway
SCIENCE AND RELIGION
    Thomas Dixon and Adam R. Shapiro
SCIENCE FICTION David Seed
THE SCIENTIFIC REVOLUTION
    Lawrence M. Principe
SCOTLAND Rab Houston
SECULARISM Andrew Copson
SEXUAL SELECTION Marlene Zuk and
    Leigh W. Simmons
SEXUALITY Véronique Mottier
WILLIAM SHAKESPEARE
    Stanley Wells
SHAKESPEARE'S COMEDIES
    Bart van Es
SHAKESPEARE'S SONNETS AND
    POEMS Jonathan F. S. Post
SHAKESPEARE'S TRAGEDIES
    Stanley Wells
GEORGE BERNARD SHAW
    Christopher Wixson
MARY SHELLEY Charlotte Gordon
THE SHORT STORY Andrew Kahn
SIKHISM Eleanor Nesbitt
SILENT FILM Donna Kornhaber
THE SILK ROAD James A. Millward

SLANG Jonothon Green
SLEEP Steven W. Lockley and
    Russell G. Foster
SMELL Matthew Cobb
ADAM SMITH Christopher J. Berry
SOCIAL AND CULTURAL
    ANTHROPOLOGY
    John Monaghan and Peter Just
SOCIAL PSYCHOLOGY Richard J. Crisp
SOCIAL WORK Sally Holland and
    Jonathan Scourfield
SOCIALISM Michael Newman
SOCIOLINGUISTICS John Edwards
SOCIOLOGY Steve Bruce
SOCRATES C. C. W. Taylor
SOFT MATTER Tom McLeish
SOUND Mike Goldsmith
SOUTHEAST ASIA James R. Rush
THE SOVIET UNION Stephen Lovell
THE SPANISH CIVIL WAR
    Helen Graham
SPANISH LITERATURE Jo Labanyi
THE SPARTANS Andrew J. Bayliss
SPINOZA Roger Scruton
SPIRITUALITY Philip Sheldrake
SPORT Mike Cronin
STARS Andrew King
STATISTICS David J. Hand
STEM CELLS Jonathan Slack
STOICISM Brad Inwood
STRUCTURAL ENGINEERING
    David Blockley
STUART BRITAIN John Morrill
SUBURBS Carl Abbott
THE SUN Philip Judge
SUPERCONDUCTIVITY
    Stephen Blundell
SUPERSTITION Stuart Vyse
SYMMETRY Ian Stewart
SYNAESTHESIA Julia Simner
SYNTHETIC BIOLOGY Jamie A. Davies
SYSTEMS BIOLOGY Eberhard O. Voit
TAXATION Stephen Smith
TEETH Peter S. Ungar
TERRORISM Charles Townshend
THEATRE Marvin Carlson
THEOLOGY David F. Ford
THINKING AND REASONING
    Jonathan St B. T. Evans
THOUGHT Tim Bayne

TIBETAN BUDDHISM
    Matthew T. Kapstein
TIDES David George Bowers and
    Emyr Martyn Roberts
TIME Jenann Ismael
TOCQUEVILLE Harvey C. Mansfield
LEO TOLSTOY Liza Knapp
TOPOLOGY Richard Earl
TRAGEDY Adrian Poole
TRANSLATION Matthew Reynolds
THE TREATY OF VERSAILLES
    Michael S. Neiberg
TRIGONOMETRY
    Glen Van Brummelen
THE TROJAN WAR Eric H. Cline
TRUST Katherine Hawley
THE TUDORS John Guy
TWENTIETH-CENTURY BRITAIN
    Kenneth O. Morgan
TYPOGRAPHY Paul Luna
THE UNITED NATIONS
    Jussi M. Hanhimäki
UNIVERSITIES AND COLLEGES
    David Palfreyman and Paul Temple
THE U.S. CIVIL WAR Louis P. Masur
THE U.S. CONGRESS Donald A. Ritchie
THE U.S. CONSTITUTION
    David J. Bodenhamer
THE U.S. SUPREME COURT
    Linda Greenhouse
UTILITARIANISM
    Katarzyna de Lazari-Radek and
    Peter Singer
UTOPIANISM Lyman Tower Sargent
VATICAN II Shaun Blanchard and
    Stephen Bullivant
VETERINARY SCIENCE James Yeates
THE VICTORIANS Martin Hewitt
THE VIKINGS Julian D. Richards
VIOLENCE Philip Dwyer
THE VIRGIN MARY
    Mary Joan Winn Leith
THE VIRTUES Craig A. Boyd and
    Kevin Timpe
VIRUSES Dorothy H. Crawford
VOLCANOES Michael J. Branney and
    Jan Zalasiewicz
VOLTAIRE Nicholas Cronk
WAR AND RELIGION Jolyon Mitchell
    and Joshua Rey

WAR AND TECHNOLOGY
    Alex Roland
WATER John Finney
WAVES Mike Goldsmith
WEATHER Storm Dunlop
THE WELFARE STATE David Garland
WITCHCRAFT Malcolm Gaskill
WITTGENSTEIN A. C. Grayling
WORK Stephen Fineman
WORLD MUSIC Philip Bohlman

WORLD MYTHOLOGY David Leeming
THE WORLD TRADE
    ORGANIZATION
    Amrita Narlikar
WORLD WAR II Gerhard L. Weinberg
WRITING AND SCRIPT
    Andrew Robinson
ZIONISM Michael Stanislawski
ÉMILE ZOLA Brian Nelson

Available soon:

CIVIL WARS Monica Duffy Toft
THE GULAG Alan Barenberg

SIMONE WEIL Rebecca Rozelle-Stone
DOSTOEVSKY Deborah Martinsen

For more information visit our website

www.oup.com/vsi/

Sabrina Ragone and Guido Smorto

COMPARATIVE
LAW

A Very Short Introduction

OXFORD
UNIVERSITY PRESS

Great Clarendon Street, Oxford, OX2 6DP,
United Kingdom

Oxford University Press is a department of the University of Oxford.
It furthers the University's objective of excellence in research, scholarship,
and education by publishing worldwide. Oxford is a registered trade mark of
Oxford University Press in the UK and in certain other countries

Published in the United States of America by Oxford University Press
198 Madison Avenue, New York, NY 10016, United States of America

British Library Cataloguing in Publication Data
Data available

Library of Congress Control Number: 2023938859

ISBN 978-0-19-289339-0

Printed by Integrated Books International, United States of America

Contents

Note on the text xvii

List of illustrations xix

1   What is comparative law? 1

2   Classifying legal systems 18

3   Legal traditions 38

4   Methods and approaches 67

5   Sameness and difference 92

6   What for? The uses of comparative law 107

7   An evolving field 127

References and further reading 131

Index 143

Note on the text

This book has been conceived and written jointly by the co-authors. Sabrina Ragone has drafted Chapters 1, 3, and 6. Guido Smorto has drafted Chapters 2, 4, 5, and 7.

List of illustrations

1 The 1900 Paris World
  Exhibition's main entrance **2**
  National Gallery of Art

2 Jeanne Chauvin, the first
  French female lawyer **4**
  Bridgeman Images

3 Illustration of Wigmore's
  'Kaleidoscope of Justice' **20**
  John H. Wigmore

4 Portrait of Irnerius, the
  renowned medieval jurist **58**
  Heritage Image Partnership Ltd /
  Alamy Stock Photo

5 'Trial of a Sow and Pigs at
  Lavegny' **80**
  Christine Kohler

6 Ranking of business
  regulation in 190
  economies **87**
  World Bank Group, Doing Business
  Database

Chapter 1
What is comparative law?

At the dawning of the 20th century, universalism, openness to other cultures, and faith in progress were the driving visions of society. The Paris World Exhibition held in 1900 (Figure 1), one of the major world's fairs in history, hosted more than fifty million visitors. Dozens of countries around the globe gathered to share their culture and accomplishments, and to celebrate the achievements of the previous century while preparing for the future. Artistic innovations (Art Nouveau), new means of transportation (the first line of the Paris metro), and architectural masterpieces (Petit and Grand Palais) were either reserved or built for this exhibition. From electricity to the new cinematograph, invented by the Lumière brothers, several technological innovations of major importance were displayed for the first time. An important world chess tournament was played involving the best players from the United States, the United Kingdom, the Russian Empire, Austria-Hungary, the German Empire, France, and Cuba.

The second modern Summer Olympic Games were also held in Paris in 1900. Twenty-eight nations, 1,000 athletes, and, for the first time ever, twenty-two women took part in the event. The Swiss sailor Hélène de Pourtalès was awarded the first gold medal as a crewmember of the winning team in the 1–2 ton sailing event,

1. **The 1900 Paris World Exhibition's main entrance (Porte Monumentale).**

and the English tennis player Charlotte Cooper was the first woman to obtain the individual title of Olympic champion.

A comparable *Zeitgeist* affected law. The same year, Paris was also the venue of the First International Congress of Comparative Law, the event that is widely considered to be the conventional establishment of comparative law as a discipline. A similar spirit of universalism, inclusiveness, and openness towards foreign cultures and traditions inspired the Congress. Experts gathered to discuss the nature, targets, and methodology of legal comparison and, no less important, to investigate how to achieve a set of universal, unifying principles. By translating the foreign into the familiar, comparative law promised to make these universal principles apparent by helping to delineate a 'common law for the civilized world', as stated by Raymond Saleilles, the main organizer of the Congress and one of the founding figures of those 'jurists inquiets' who played a pivotal role in the critique of what represented the epitome of strict national positivism, the École de l'Exégèse.

If the Congress of Paris set the theoretical foundations of comparative scholarship, the practical vocation of comparative law was especially emphasized at the Universal Congress of Lawyers and Jurists held four years later in St Louis, Missouri, the founding act of comparative law in the United States. The Congress was soon followed by the establishment of the Comparative Law Bureau within the American Bar Association, which founded the *Annual Bulletin*, the first comparative law journal in the United States, with the aim of providing legal data and scholarship from several countries, ranging from Belgium, Germany, Spain, and Switzerland to Japan and Latin America. These initiatives were particularly aimed at practitioners (rather than academics) interested in legal activities with a transnational dimension.

Openness involved legal professions as well, in a similar way as happened with sports. In December 1900, Olga Petit and Jeanne Chauvin (Figure 2) were the first women in France to take their oath as lawyers, a few decades after the US had taken the same step.

Still, as Chapter 2 will address, laws used to be (and mainly are) adopted and implemented at the national level. Therefore, the second dimension in the development of legal comparison, alongside openness and universalism, was the attention paid to domestic norms. In fact, comparing national laws was considered for a long time to be the core business of comparative studies.

A relatively young comparative discipline

In principle, comparative law encompasses the following operations: the comparative assessment of entire legal systems or specific laws, regulations, judgements and customs in order to

2. Jeanne Chauvin, the first French female lawyer.

unveil similarities and differences; the study of how legal solutions are imitated, transplanted, accepted, and rejected in other countries or social groups; and the methodological issues arising from the study of different legal systems, families, and traditions (see Chapters 2 and 3). In this respect, according to methodologists like Rodolfo Sacco, the mere study of foreign law does not amount to proper comparison, but instead it becomes a phase within the realization of a comparative study. Nonetheless, there are authors who do include pieces on foreign law under the umbrella of legal comparison, as they would require the scholar to employ a distinct methodological toolkit in order to understand the norms of another system or tradition.

To a certain extent, comparative law has existed in a broader sense since Montesquieu's contributions in the 18th century and even since Aristotle's *Politics* classifying numerous real and imaginary 'constitutions' of city-states. Nevertheless, as an academic discipline, it was a latecomer with respect to other legal fields with an international dimension, such as public international law (the norms governing the relationships between sovereign states and international organizations), and private international law (the norms used to solve disputes or govern situations, such as contracts or marriages, involving citizens or corporations of various states). In contrast to international (public and private) law, this new field was not intended to designate a positive body of rules but rather an approach to norms, institutions, or entire legal systems belonging to different social and geographical contexts, with the aim of grasping similarities and differences.

Comparative law was also a latecomer with respect to other comparative disciplines. As a scientific method, comparison is nothing new, as explained by Dirk Berg-Schlosser. In the 15th century, Cardinal Cusanus claimed that all research was pursued by establishing comparative relations, and in subsequent centuries as well, comparison was considered a universal method. From natural sciences like comparative biology to sciences that explore similarities and dissimilarities of cultural and social phenomena, such as philology, anthropology, or politics, comparison became an established method of study. In the 19th century, the fields of linguistics, religion, and folklore represented the paradigm of comparative studies.

In particular, comparative linguistics gained momentum when European linguists started to investigate a new language family, the 'Indo-European' (as named by Sir Thomas Young), after they discovered that Sanskrit presented similarities with Greek, Latin, Persian, and ancient German. The application of this methodology favoured the elaboration of classifications based on family trees, explaining the genetic interconnections between languages and proto-languages. The establishment of philology as a historical and comparative science showed how to extrapolate a model by taking into account different languages, their origin and their cultural transmission. The hermeneutics behind the logical operation of comparing words and roots from distinct languages is similar to that used in comparative legal scholarship.

Drawing inspiration from his background of comparative linguistics, Friedrich Max Müller, who taught in Oxford during the second half of the century, determined the institution of comparative religion. This academic discipline also aimed to study religions from a comparative perspective to shed light on the roots, diffusion, and migration of doctrines and beliefs.

Therefore, the 19th century shaped the concepts of classic and primitive, and then exotic and modern, somehow drawing borders which separated the West from the rest of the world as well as the other way around. The political implications of this approach are significant and can be seen in phenomena such as legal and cultural imperialism, with colonizers imposing their law on the conquered territories, or more recently, with Western countries aiming to export their democratic standards.

Not unlike the archetypical comparative sciences, comparative politics and other comparative social sciences seek to provide general theories on the forces leading to change and evolutionary trends in political and social systems depending on economic, social, and historical factors. Inductively, they elaborate on tendencies, causality, and path dependence, and use comparison as a sort of 'experiment' for the testing of these theories.

Between theory and practice

The previously mentioned two-fold dimension, combining purely theoretical purposes and practical targets aimed at international integration and conflict resolution, among others, is at the core of comparative law as a discipline (see Chapter 6). The theoretical dimension, emphasized by comparativists of all generations, underlines the role of legal comparison in the better understanding of legal data, their explanation and classification for purposes of knowledge. The practical dimension encompasses the use by founding fathers and legislators in drafting constitutions and laws, the inclusion of foreign law within judicial reasoning, the achievement of common norms in international or supranational realms, as well as the realization of proper legal translations.

Comparative law enhances cultural and critical skills. Many of the masters of comparative law were prominent figures in the fight against legal positivism and formalism that were at the centre of all debates in both the United States and Europe at the time. This is why legal comparison is relevant not only for scholars interested in foreign law but also for domestic academics and practitioners. The study of legal institutions and traditions of other countries helps us to develop a more critical take on our own legal system.

At the same time, comparative law has always aimed at being useful for the achievement of practical, programmatic targets as well. This was already the case at the beginning of the 20th century, as the experience of Ernst Rabel for instance proves: he was the co-founder of the first University Institute for Comparative Law in Germany in Munich, but he also served as a judge on several international judicial bodies and was a member of the International Institute for the Unification of Private Law (UNIDROIT), fostering the unification of rules for international sales transactions. It is certainly true in times of globalization and integration among states. Solving, instead of simply analysing, the problems of managing difference has become a task for modern lawyers seeking to understand foreign legal institutions and tackle them effectively.

In fact, in its short history, comparative law has served different missions. Countless projects of unification and harmonization of law have been pursued with the help of comparative analysis, deserving of both praise and criticism (see Chapter 5), with the objective of introducing identical norms or principles in different countries through international and supranational legislation. Primarily aimed at favouring trade and commercial relations through the creation of an international 'common law', these projects have pursued the most diverse purposes, such as maintaining peace, assisting international institution building, improving legal drafting, fighting the Cold War, aiding decolonization, or providing guidance to foster modernization (whatever that may mean).

The achievement of legal convergence to aid trade and commercial purposes proves the point. For instance, the European Economic Community, founded by the Treaty of Rome in 1957 for the achievement of economic integration, required the adoption of common and harmonized rules among the member states for the realization of a common market and a customs union. A shared set of rules was needed to eliminate internal borders and regulatory obstacles for the free movement of goods and services. These foundations easily explain the use of comparative law in the development of what is now European Union law and the jurisprudence of the Court of Justice of the EU. On a global scale, the World Trade Organization promotes free multilateral trade, reinforcing principles such as transparency and fairness. Bilateral and multilateral trade agreements are equally based on the achievement of uniform standards to favour mutual investments and contractual relations.

A relativistic and humble approach to the law

More than any other legal field, comparative law, pursuing the innovative ambition of challenging the national boundaries of legal analysis, needed to elaborate both theoretical and methodological aspects of the discipline. In particular, it had to focus on definitions, categories, and methods in order to find an appropriate vocabulary to identify this new approach to the study of law. It also had to challenge the legal mindset of domestic scholars who were accustomed to thinking about the law as it was in their own countries.

The first, foundational issue of comparative analysis concerns the identification of what 'law' is in different legal systems and traditions. An elected parliament may perform the law-making function that in another system is assigned to the judiciary, or to the community. This diversity may constitute a primary difficulty for comparative analyses. Not only do legal systems recognize different sources of law, but they also give them a different weight and value. Understanding what kinds of sources a jurisdiction acknowledges and how it handles them is of the utmost importance for any comparative inquiry. It can also bring major difficulties. For instance, understanding legal traditions based on the oral transmission of rules can be complex for Western scholars. Similarly, experts in religious traditions struggle to embrace the secular conception of the law, which is enforced in other systems.

Therefore, comparativists must get rid of their previously acquired legal mindset and make the effort to enter into that of the 'others'. They have to appreciate what domestic jurists of another country would consider as sources of law, applying that country's domestic criteria to interpret and systematize them. This strategy is not as easy as it may seem at first glance. Comparativists embrace a relativistic approach, entering into the logic of the other studied systems without prejudices or preconceptions. Additionally, in a sense they need to become legally 'agnostic' and accept that there is no proper, perfect legal solution, but that there are appropriate solutions depending on time, space, and context. For example, most societies punish murder with imprisonment, whereas some indigenous groups interpret this offence as a challenge to the group's harmony and punish the guilty parties by laying on them the obligation to serve the family of the victim and their community. Such punishments reflect the worldview of the interested social groups, and no hierarchy among legal solutions is possible for comparativists.

European continental scholars may have been the least suitable for addressing other traditions since they were raised with the positivistic belief in the existence of complete, comprehensive, and internally consistent legal systems in the wake of codifications. This ideology defended a conception of legal sources according to which the law is created through codes and legislation, forming a gapless system of legal propositions. While decisive in understanding a legal system, cases and scholarly writings are not deemed to be sources of law. From a positivistic viewpoint, judicial decisions are the mere application of an abstract legal rule to a factual situation through means of legal logic. In other words, judges apply the rules, and legal scholarship comments upon and clarifies their meaning. Of course, divergences in interpretation cannot be excluded. However, when identical statutory rules bring two courts to different judicial decisions, one decision may be considered erroneous and therefore shall be overruled by a higher judge who is entitled to provide a more correct interpretation of the norm. This reconstruction becomes untenable in a comparative analysis. If a Portuguese statute contains the same phrasing as a Spanish statute, but the corresponding judges interpret them differently, it would not make sense to say that Portuguese judges are right and the Spanish wrong, without taking into account the context that led to the respective interpretations.

France, Italy, and many other Western systems share a similar view of the sources of law. Comparable similarities equate Common Law systems that allot significant law-making power to judges, making it easier for a US scholar to study Canadian or Australian law. More substantial difficulties, and very interesting challenges, arise when the foreign law responds to a different logic in which legal norms cannot be separated from ethics, morals, and religion.

Originally comparative law was mainly based on Western standards, labelling the rest of the world's canons as exotic or less developed. Of course, perceptions change dramatically over time. In medieval times, when 'Asia was the world' (in the words of Stewart Gordon), European customs, scientific achievements, and commercial habits seemed much less developed to Asian observers and travellers. The rhetoric of liberation used by Napoleon when invading Egypt was deemed fake and self-serving by local scholars, criticizing the imposition of alien rules and heavy burdens on their society. Even today, when observing Western laws in practice, 'the rest' notice their inconsistencies, hypocrisies, and cracking legitimacy, as Laura Nader has explained.

The progressive inclusion and understanding of legal traditions further away from the West have led comparativists to take into due consideration not only statutes but also judgements and scholarship. Therefore, comparative analyses adopt a realistic, bottom-up perspective, investigating which actors, institutions, or events produce legal norms in each system. Elements like oral traditions, religious interpretations, trade usages, contractual standard terms, social mechanisms, and customs, which would not amount to official legal sources according to Western orthodoxy, should be included in the picture as long as they determine the meaning and scope of the legal norms under consideration.

Even more impalpable aspects, including underlying theories and conceptions, tacit assumptions, legal culture, and the language of a foreign legal system, are crucial. For instance, according to conventional accounts, anyone wishing to establish a business relationship should remember to greet the oldest person first when dealing with Chinese partners, or to hold and deliver important documents with both hands if the company is Japanese. In order to grasp those extra-legal factors that affect the law, comparative studies have to assess and understand structural aspects, such as political power, economic hegemony, cultural legitimacy, rhetorical elements, shared beliefs, and ways of thinking. From this perspective, law is seen as a social, contextual phenomenon that evolves and changes over time, and thus is subject to constant amendments.

As a consequence, comparative law embraces a humble approach which does not rely exclusively on legal assumptions and knowledge. Such a comprehensive approach to legal sources and the consequent appraisal of legal systems in their entirety require a truly interdisciplinary approach. History, sociology, anthropology, political science, economics (to name a few) cannot be underestimated when trying to identify the roots and targets of a foreign norm. One cannot study a parliamentary system without understanding equilibria among political parties; or grasp the meaning of a norm on gender equality without consulting statistical data on women's representation.

Therefore, comparative law makes use of different disciplines which provide insightful knowledge on the legal systems analysed. Of course, the level of interdisciplinarity and the choice of the other sciences to include depend on the specific topic examined. Language and linguistics are paramount for the study and understanding of foreign norms, while history provides the essential reconstruction of facts and events for the comparativist to appreciate the origin and development of any legal institution. Political science can complement the traditionally prevalent object of legal studies, i.e., the 'law in books', offering explanations of the 'law in action', such as when the comparativist approaches political systems, presidential powers, political parties, and so on. Sociology as well can offer insights into the relationship between a society and its corresponding legal system. Let's just imagine the study of the recognition of indigenous groups within a given legal system. From this perspective, anthropology has turned increasingly important as comparative legal studies have become more inclusive, frequently now addressing non-Western forms of producing norms and organizing societies. Necessarily, depending on the topic, further disciplines may be relevant, from legal theory to philosophy, economics, statistics, geography, and even psychology or medicine. Consequently, comparative law is characterized by methodological openness to other fields to achieve a greater understanding and contextualization of foreign rules.

Foreign law as a subject of study

Studying foreign law requires a comprehensive, open-minded approach. The mindset is similar to that of travellers, as Günter Frankenberg remarked: 'The traveller and the comparatist are invited to break away from daily routines, to meet the unexpected and, perhaps, to get to know the unknown.'

The comparative endeavour entails three basic phases: study, understanding, and comparison of the norms being analysed. The first and second phases acquire particular relevance when approaching foreign law. One cannot take for granted a foreign rule, as one might if it belonged to one's own system. Foreign law must be addressed in its entirety, not focusing exclusively on the specific issue at stake. Otherwise, comparativists run the risk of searching in the wrong legal field or in the wrong source. For instance, they may look for the regulation of a certain right in the country's constitution when it is actually located in its statutes or regulations. Also, interpretations given to rules in practice have to be assessed, and the authority in charge may vary according to the system analysed. Ideally, one should take into account the social, political, historical, and economic contexts in order to fully understand the rationale and targets of each foreign rule.

In this respect, language plays a paramount role as an element of facilitation or complication. Specialist bilingual dictionaries or dictionaries giving an explanation based on one's own system would be particularly useful for comparative endeavours.

Translations as well could be extremely beneficial in legal comparisons, but they are not always available and reliable. In fact, as also addressed in Chapter 4, the name of a specific institution may be different or misleading in other systems. Provinces are local entities in Spain and Italy, while they are member states of federal countries in Canada or Argentina. Comparing them would simply restate the obvious and would imply methodological flaws in the selection of the cases. The Northern European *ombudsman* corresponds to the so-called *defensor del pueblo* in other parts of the world. In other cases, foreign legal terms do not have an exact translation into other languages, such as the Anglo-Saxon contract of 'trust'.

Even when different legal systems make use of similar words or concepts, their actual meaning can be and often is significantly divergent. For example, an institution like marriage, whose denomination can be common to many countries, may be applicable to distinct sets of situations, spanning from opposite-sex and/or same-sex relationships, polygamy, child marriages, and forced marriages. This is true today, and even more so if one analyses the regulation of marriage from a comparative historical perspective.

Another example of the importance of a comprehensive approach is the potential comparative study of the scope of free speech in the US and in Europe. Theoretical reconstructions prove that, over time, the First Amendment of the US constitution has provided extensive protection for free speech, including cases that from the European viewpoint would amount to discriminatory manifestations. The 'marketplace of ideas' metaphor, often attributed to John Stuart Mill's essay *On Liberty* (1859), justifies these limitations of censorship and restraints and encourages the free flow of ideas. It relies on a market-based conception and claims that the truthfulness or acceptance of opinions rests on the outcome of their mutual competition, exempt from the control of any authority. It was first invoked by Justice Oliver Wendell

Holmes in 1919 and then applied by the Supreme Court copious times, setting a very high bar for any prohibition or sanction of thought and expression.

This bar seems (formally) much lower in most European countries. Nevertheless, although legal texts apparently allow for a wider scope of freedom of speech in the US than in the Old Continent, this merely doctrinal approach to the law would lead us to obviate or underestimate numerous social and contextual elements which actually constrain public speech, thus reducing the scope of what is considered 'socially acceptable' in America.

Major difficulties and precautions

Comparative law used to be subject to criticism with respect to its lack of geographical comprehensiveness, since an assessment of all areas of law, in all jurisdictions, would be unattainable and was not even attempted at first. Nevertheless, phenomena like globalization, Europeanization, and the spread of international legal instruments involving different countries have revived the theoretical and practical discussions on the selection of case studies. This field has defended its value as an autonomous academic discipline. Engaging in comparative endeavours involves the same search for knowledge and cultural enrichment as that of any other legal field, providing a validation to legal comparison without a distinctive need for justification. It contributes to the understanding of how legal solutions are elaborated and copied, succeed or fail, and how legal families and traditions coexist, clash, or influence each other.

Comparative law has had to become less 'Western oriented' and more inclusive, giving wider space to areas of the world often neglected by traditional scholars. The 'Global South critique' to comparative studies exemplifies the matter, as it requires the opening of comparative legal scholarship beyond the so-called Global North. For decades, mainstream scholarship dealt with only a few countries, like the United States, the United Kingdom, France, or Germany, supposedly covering all (relevant) legal reality. The cases to include in comparative inquiries would be a few prosperous, stable democracies of the Global North—the 'usual suspects', as Ran Hirschl names them—as if they were representative of the world's diversity.

Of course, depending on the topic, the set of country cases will vary. Not all comparative assessment needs to include the entire world, but it cannot be blind to non-Western traditions. The selection of relevant case studies, in fact, is pivotal in legitimizing and giving substance to each comparison. The accusation of strategic 'cherry-picking' will always be there, and it can be moved against all judges or legislators who only quote norms consistent with their own particular *desiderata*, and even more so against scholars who are seen to choose countries that fit with their previous knowledge, expertise, or even career prospects. Therefore, the justifications used in the choice of cases become vital, along with the explanation of the target pursued by the individual inquiry. Theoretical assessments of models, imitations, or transplants do not require the same skills or the same methodological approaches.

Scholars, judges, legislators, and lawyers interested in other legal systems should be able to obtain reliable information. Ideally, they should use primary sources, i.e., original documents written in that country's language. However, in some cases they can also rely on secondary sources, such as official translations or studies on that system. Comprehensive studies covering numerous countries, for instance, will necessarily lead the comparativist to use secondary sources as one may not be fluent in all the languages involved, nor have direct access to all the relevant data. The increasing availability of official information helps in this. With the evolution of methodology the need has been reinforced for comparativists to enter into the mentality of other systems, avoiding judgemental attitudes and prejudices.

In spite of the difficulties, through the proper methodology, legal comparison can fulfil rigorous standards, becoming a powerful educational tool and a practical aid in law-making. One of the major analytical aims of comparative law has been, and is, to group legal data into different categories, providing a systematic ordering of legal knowledge through classifications which are useful for teaching, studying, and comparing. This is why classification is one of the keywords of the field.

Chapter 2
Classifying legal systems

The rise of the nation-state and the birth of comparative law

At the dawn of the 20th century, state sovereignty is the driving principle in politics and law. In politics, the transition to particularism that has taken place since the Treaty of Westphalia is complete and Europe is divided into nation-states. In law, a new legal order has supplanted that of the Middle Ages based on a common law (*ius commune*) for Europe. State law is the only binding law and any form of non-state normativity that might affect the unity of the state is banned. Within national borders, the many non-state actors and alternative forms of regulation that shaped the law during the Middle Ages—e.g., merchant law, canon law—are regarded as non-laws or are incorporated into national law. Beyond national borders, national legal systems are considered to be autonomous and sovereign entities shielded from foreign influence, with relationships between them conceptualized as inherently conflictual ('conflict of laws' is the name given to the nascent branch of international law that regulates divergences in national laws).

A new legal mythology justifies this framework. The law of each nation is seen as a coherent, complete, and unified body of rules, hierarchically ordered and free from gaps. In continental Europe, this legalistic tendency leads to regarding the monarchs as legislators and considering legislation to be the only source of law to be mechanically applied by the courts. The only activity an interpreter could perform is a strict *exegesis* of statutory law, a term derived from the interpretation of the Holy Scriptures to depict a passive attitude to an authoritative text. In England, the same legalistic tendency leads to the affirmation of *stare decisis* ('let the decisions stand'). This principle imposes on judges that they must abide by earlier decisions made by their predecessors, following a rule of precedent reinforced by the reorganization of the court system, which took place at the end of the 19th century. Only an Act of parliament could alter such precedents, and any departure from prior decisions would entail a usurpation of the legislative function.

The taxonomy project

Faced with this nationalization of law and legal studies, the emerging field of comparative legal studies aims to transcend national borders in the study of law, and to reject the role of lawyers as mere interpreters of national legal systems. As in other comparative studies—anatomy or linguistics—taxonomy forms a crucial part of comparative legal studies, and the systematization of the study of national legal systems is one of the main tasks of comparative law.

Gathering state laws into a limited number of types makes it possible to handle the otherwise unmanageable mass of information about national legal systems. Legal taxonomy categorizes the several legal systems of the world into a handful of 'families' based on common patterns, with each legal system seen as a member of a given family. Once this categorization is accomplished, the analysis can be limited to the general features of each family with a resulting simplification of comparative inquiries. Moreover, since conventional taxonomies postulate the likeness of the legal systems belonging to the same family, it is possible to single out the supposedly representative legal systems that shaped the family—the so-called 'parent' or 'grand' legal systems—and to compare entire families at once, with the drastic reduction of legal systems considered to be worthy objects of study. The analysis of French (or German) law can shed light on continental European law, and studying English (or American) law becomes a convenient way to appreciate Common Law as a whole.

Mapping the legal systems of the world

In the first decades of the 20th century many academics tried to classify legal systems. In most cases they employed criteria and descriptions that today look unacceptable or overly naïve: from the racial characteristics used by Georges Sauser-Hall—who identified the laws of Aryans and Indo-Europeans, Semitics, Mongolic, and 'barbarous people'—to the captivating pictorial method of John Henry Wigmore's 'Kaleidoscope of Justice' (Figure 3).

A KALEIDOSCOPE OF JUSTICE

EUROPE

ASIA

AFRICA

BASIC PATTERN

AMERICA

OCEANIA

ANCIENT PEOPLES

When the Basic Pattern Revolves, the Prisms Cause Variant Patterns in Different Communities;
But the Latent Elements Remain the Same Throughout

3. **Illustration of Wigmore's 'Kaleidoscope of Justice'.**

In the middle of the 20th century, a classification proposed by the renowned French scholar René David was rapidly taken to be the archetype of legal taxonomy and the starting point for any comparative analysis for decades to come. David grouped the legal systems of the world under four main headings. 'Romano-Germanic' designates the Civil Law of continental Europe and of those systems around the globe that were influenced by it (the term acknowledges the Roman roots and the role of legal scholars, embodied in German legal thought of the 19th century). Common Law comprises the law of England and those legal systems influenced by English law: those of the United States, Canada, Australia, and New Zealand, among others. A third, socialist family encompasses the law of the Union of Soviet Socialist Republics (USSR) and of the many socialist or people's republics of the world aimed at creating a communist society. Finally, David groups those legal systems worldwide where 'the place and function of law are very different from what they are in the West', in a last, catch-all family named 'Other Conceptions of Law and the Social Order'.

When David formulated his legal mapping of the world, Civil Law and Common Law were seen as the two most distinctive intellectual systems of law ever created. As such, they received the almost exclusive attention of comparative legal studies. David was no exception, devoting more than half of his textbook to these two families. At the same time, his contribution was crucial for refining the oversimplified account of the time, which depicted Civil Law as 'written law' based on codification, and Common Law as 'unwritten law' made up of judges' decisions. In this regard, David offered a more nuanced perspective by emphasizing the importance of history in the formation of the fundamental features of each family based on their common roots.

David traced the birth of Civil Law to the rise of a vulgarized form of ancient Roman law (*ius commune*) during the Middle Ages that was treated as the law of the land across continental Europe.

Lacking a unifying political power, a European class of academic scholars started to interpret and adapt the *Corpus Iuris Civilis*—the Roman Emperor Justinian's compilation, which was rediscovered around the year 1100—to the needs of the times. Its academic origin explains why Civil Law typically displays a strong tendency towards systematization and abstraction. This distinctive feature has been preserved even after the end of the medieval legal order when legislation replaced academic writings as the primary source of law. The codification movement that took place under the influence of 18th-century rationalism epitomizes this tendency for systematization. Codes are considered to be a comprehensive, coherent, and closely integrated body of rules that encompass entire areas of national law (e.g., private law, criminal law, procedure, etc.) in a logically closed system without gaps. The style of legal reasoning mirrors this ideal. Judges make deductive applications of general rules before a pending case, using a syllogism to apply the appropriate statutory rule to the particular facts of the case under scrutiny in order to reach the only logical conclusion. In this framework, lacunae in the legislative text are only apparent, and are filled in by way of interpretation. No rule exists that judges should follow judicial precedents. Prior court decisions are relevant only as offering an interpretation of written law, but they have no binding authority, and they cannot be taken as providing the grounds for new decisions.

On the opposite side of the spectrum David puts Common Law, which he depicts as sharply dissimilar from Civil Law. He traces the birth of Common Law to the particular political and legal organization that Norman kings set up in England after their conquest in the 11th century. The bulk of decisions that the King's courts made during centuries gave rise to a judge-made law 'common to all free men of the realm'. Due to this judicial origin, Common Law leaves no room for abstract generalities, and it displays quite distinctive techniques for drafting and interpreting legal rules. Almost immune from Roman influence, it developed its own unique legal concepts, categories, and vocabulary which reflect the greater importance of procedure and evidence, with judges who are more concerned with remedies than substantive rules. In this framework, conceptual order and logical systematizations have never been key ambitions, and applying the law is regarded more as a craft than as a science based on logic. Here, rules are a means for resolving disputes rather than a set of general rules of conduct, and they are formulated in narrow statements with regard to a peculiar set of facts. Correspondingly, judges do not frame the case in abstract terms in order to apply the proper set of general rules to the case under scrutiny. Instead, they reason from the material facts of prior cases to extrapolate the rules. During the 19th century, a rule of precedent was developed to govern such inductive reasoning and give certainty and stability to the law, with courts obliged to follow prior decisions. The practical system for training and recruiting judges, and the style of statutory rules corroborate this pragmatic approach.

While David depicts the distinction between Civil Law and Common Law as being primarily technical, he identifies more radical differences between these first two families and the others, based on the different role of law in governing society. When he first wrote his successful treatise, the law of the USSR and those countries that adhered to Marxist doctrine and looked to the USSR for guidance was of the greatest interest for legal comparison. Emerging from the 1917 Bolshevik Revolution in Russia, the distinguishing feature of this family was its subordination to Marxism-Leninism and its political goal, that is, the building of a communist society where exploitation and class antagonism will finally end and a fraternal society will emerge. In this type of society, there would be no need for state or law. Only moral rules, customs, social duties, and basic precepts of economic organizations would survive. However, a political transition is indispensable in order to achieve this goal. The revolutionary work of the legislature, guided by the Communist Party in accordance with the basic principles of Marxism-Leninism, directs this passage from the revolution to the new society. As a result, despite the professed goal of having a society with no state and no law, state and law remained crucial for governing economic activities and shaping people's conscience during the transitory socialist stage. The need for a planned economy, where all means of production are collectivized, and the task of educating individuals for a future world, made rules far more pervasive than in capitalist countries, and violations of the principles of 'socialist legality' a fundamental threat to the transition to a new social order. The socialist family will never achieve this idealized communist society and the transitory socialist stage in fact lasted until the fall of the Berlin Wall and the collapse of the Soviet Union.

Aside from the three 'principal' legal families, David groups all non-Western societies into one catch-all, residual legal family, in which he distinguishes two main sub-groups. The first includes those legal systems where the law is related to a religion or a particular view of social order. In these societies, law is not only recognized as a rule of conduct but also idealized. Rules are 'unorganised, fragmentary and unstable' compared to Western laws, and 'there is a general feeling that true law is to be found elsewhere than in legislation, custom or judicial decisions'. Hindu, Jewish, and especially Muslim law exemplify this group of legal systems. As an example, Muslim law is not separate from the religion, and the rules of *Sharia* are not made by humans but revealed by God. The state in Muslim countries does not only govern the society but serves the revealed religion.

The second sub-group of the residual family embraces those legal systems that reject the notion of law as arbitrary and as a factor of disorder, and govern social relationships with 'extra-legal' tools. Parts of Africa and the Far East, especially China, are pinpointed as exemplary cases of these societies. In all these systems, law is not central to social order and justice, and legal rules are only for barbarians. They may intimidate people, and they can be conveniently used when other means for resolving conflicts and re-establishing social order fail, but they do not provide a genuine model of justice. Often, these systems are said to value reconciliation over justice and mediation over litigation before courts. Their principal objective is 'the maintenance or restoration of harmony rather than respect for law', as in traditional Chinese law, whose main goal is to live within Confucianism's fundamental principles and rites.

A critique

For a long time, the foundational work by David, together with the largely analogous proposal made by the German scholars Konrad Zweigert and Hein Kötz, looked like a clear description of the world's laws. Comparativists could rely on these classifications and use them as the undisputed starting point for their research. It was only in the last part of the 20th century that the tides changed, and comparative lawyers started to see this framework as being untenable.

In the first place, critical historical reasons called for a revision of David's taxonomy that would be in line with the new geopolitical map of the world. Above all, the demise of the Soviet Empire and socialist law after the fall of the Berlin Wall made the socialist family out of date. More generally, David's classification is blamed for the almost exclusive attention paid to Western legal tradition and for the neglect of non-Western legal systems. Despite encompassing most of the world, the last residual family received only minor attention, and it is examined in much less detail than the others, often relying upon deep-rooted stereotypes. The end of the Iron Curtain and the increasing awareness of non-Western laws brought into question the accuracy of such a 'Euro-American centric' taxonomy and called for more inclusive, less colonial ways of mapping the laws of the world, which would include Asian, Latin American, and African systems in comparative inquiries.

Remarkably, this accusation of Western bias does not just entail a call for more attention to these non-Western laws. More radically, the conventional taxonomy project is under attack for being grounded on a Western concept of law, employed to classify the entire world by its own criteria, with any systems that do not fit this artificial ordering relegated to the margins. In this vein, David's and other conventional classifications have been accused of 'legal scientism', for being based on an objective description that is built on apparently clear lines of demarcation between legal systems and families, following a permanent set of criteria. The attempt to categorize legal systems in terms of mutual exclusivity is seen as fallacious. Grouping national legal systems as isolated members of well-defined groups is simply pointless because laws cannot be sorted to fit clearly defined categories. Moreover, this way of fixing the objects of classification assumes that legal families and legal systems are static and unchanging entities that can be categorized according to their present characteristics, in a way that does not consider possible deviations or variations.

Equally, the taxonomy project has been criticized for its 'legal nationalism'. Despite having the ambition to transcend state laws, traditional scholarship did not question the premise that national legal systems are the basic units for comparison. Like the other conventional classifications of the time, David considered national legal systems as the natural and only object to study, classify, and group into families. But the growing recognition of supranational and sub-national laws, often in tension with national law, challenges this state-centred approach to comparison. Excluding laws that are not state-based or non-systemic from the realm of comparative analysis is increasingly seen as an unacceptable simplification and as creating a major pitfall for the discipline. Moreover, the division between parent and derived legal systems is blamed for considering some systems as deserving more attention than others. This distinction entails an indefensible hierarchy, with parent systems deemed as being more 'significant' than derivative systems that 'do not possess to the same degree that blend of originality and balanced maturity', as Zweigert and Kötz put it.

From legal families to legal traditions

A more open-ended and inclusive understanding of laws is needed to replace the outdated 'Country and Western' tradition of comparative studies, as William Twining termed it, and to emphasize law's interconnected and dynamic nature. With the aim of purging classifications of their Western bias, comparativists try to redefine the conventional classifications by putting the accent on the multicultural dimension of law. As one such example, Ugo Mattei has formulated a legal taxonomy by distinguishing three ideal types. In his attempt to avoid viewing legal systems and legal families as static, and to reconceptualize them in accordance with their dynamic and indistinct nature, he identifies three different patterns of law corresponding to the leading systems of social organization: professional, political, and traditional. These three patterns interact in all legal systems. Yet, this pluralism does not forestall classification. Legal systems can still be grouped into families in accordance with the hegemony of one specific pattern and classified by the source of the social behaviour playing a leading role in them.

It is against this background that, in the last part of the 20th century, the notion of 'tradition' has supplanted that of 'family', becoming the prevailing paradigm in comparative literature, mostly thanks to the work of the Canadian scholar Patrick Glenn. In Glenn's account, local laws do not belong to one or another family. Rather, the different legal traditions of the world influence legal systems to various degrees. Bearing this in mind, a comparative analysis should not try to group legal systems as stable members of one or another family. Quite the opposite, it should identify the distinctive legal traditions of the world and investigate how, and to what degree, they shape local laws. If orthodox classifications depicted legal families as static, isolated, and mutually exclusive entities, legal traditions have a relatively stable core but no fixed boundaries. They are interconnected and overlapping, dynamic, and changing, in a continuous process of reciprocal influence.

The existence of these overlapping and shared features among legal systems and traditions suggests that all legal systems are hybrid or 'crosses'. Orthodox classifications considered legal hybrids as the exception to the norm of 'pure' legal systems and employed the term to designate those legal systems that, due to historical accidents, cannot be brought under Civil Law or Common Law, since they are influenced by both. Scotland, Louisiana, Quebec, Israel, Southern African countries, Sri Lanka, Puerto Rico, Malta, Philippines, and a few other places were seen as the most prominent examples of a *numerus clausus* of legal systems, sometimes pooled together in a distinctive legal family. With the turn from legal families to legal traditions, hybridity becomes the norm rather than the exception, and a characteristic feature of each legal system.

Likewise, all legal systems are made of different legal orders, whether official or not. An account based on the legal traditions and their variable influence on local laws better explains a world where the authority of the nation-states and formal sources of law are in decline. The term pluralism was initially employed to designate the coexistence of religious and customary laws in those legal systems where colonialists had imposed their laws on previous systems. Now, a pluralistic approach becomes essential for investigating the coexistence of different legal orders and uncovering those traditional practices that are not recognized by official law, even in those legal systems that formally recognize the state as the only law-maker and law enforcer, as in the Western world.

Comparison and legal change

Comparative law is not only aimed at describing commonalities and differences in space. Focusing on diversity and variations, it can be a powerful tool for understanding how, when, and by whom the changes in law occur, as well as to grasp the rules and patterns of legal change.

The effort to explain changes in time is common to many comparative inquiries. A comparative analysis may support historical investigations by uncovering missing documentation. Comparative linguistics could infer the existence of an undocumented common mother tongue, such as the Indo-European, by comparing known languages—Greek, Latin, Sanskrit, or Celtic—that developed from it. Similarly, by identifying similarities and differences among legal systems, legal comparison may reveal an original law, common to all the laws of a given group, that fragmented into different (often national) laws over time.

In doing this, comparative law may contribute to articulating hypotheses on the origins and the development of the law. Even more ambitiously, it may demonstrate that different societies follow similar or identical structures and formulate general theories to explain social change, uncovering those fundamental patterns which are the same in space and time due to general features common to all humanity.

Sometimes, this tendency to find general rules of development intersects with an evolutionist approach which sees any human group progressing along a predetermined and inevitable line and going through the same economic, social, and legal stages. Studies in comparative religion trace an evolution from animism to monotheism in a path from 'primitive' to 'superior' cultural models. In the same vein, this evolutionary model in law represents diversity and variations as different phases of the same path, with some societies more advanced than others, from the simplest to the most complex and sophisticated. According to this account, studying contemporary 'primitive' laws may help in understanding the historical progress of the most 'developed' Western laws and in extrapolating the history of these laws, counterbalancing the lack of historical records. For the same reason, the 'advanced' Western laws may give a hint as to what will be the future of the 'less evolved' areas in the rest of the world.

Legal transplants

Heavily criticized in anthropology, during the 20th century this evolutionistic approach lost ground in the legal field as well. A polygenetic understanding of law prevailed that questioned the existence of general patterns of development and gave a radically different explanation for legal change. Under this framework, variations and apparent similarities in law are not due to a common origin and universal patterns of development but to reciprocal influences. Imitation and diffusion better explain similarities and discontinuities in law.

Along this line, a popular theory was affirmed which complemented studies on legal change with an analysis of the historical relationships among legal systems. Coined by the Scottish historian and comparativist Alan Watson, the term 'legal transplants' started to emphasize the transmission of ideas as the most significant factor of legal change, and to show how legal systems evolve in relation to each other.

With his studies on Roman and English law, Watson traced the circulation of legal rules, institutions, and ideas across the world, providing evidence of its historical frequency and highlighting the interdependence and exchange among legal systems of the world. As he concluded, there is little genuine innovation in law.

Imitation is much more frequent, and this imitation gives rise to the transmission of legal models worldwide.

According to Watson, legal ideas and institutions endlessly travel from one place and social context to another. Legal transplants of institutions and rules are not unique and extraordinary events. Quite the opposite, they are the norm and the primary source of legal change. The circulation of Roman law across continental Europe, the influence of traditional Chinese law in Asia, the reception of Common Law in the Commonwealth, and the diffusion of Islamic law around the world, are only some of the most striking instances of this circulation. Legal transplants can be visible, open, and massive, such as the widespread adoption of the French civil code throughout the world; or they can be silent and invisible, such as the influence of the German legal sciences in Europe and beyond. They can result from top-down reforms, market-led initiatives, or judicial interpretation. They may stem from the desire to imitate supposedly 'prestigious' systems and confer an aura of respect to legal reforms, like the imitation of the Swiss civil code by Turkey; or be the result of an imposition of foreign models, such as occurred during the Napoleonic conquests or the European domination of overseas colonies.

Watson believes that the striking frequency of legal transplants lies in their ease. Legal transplants are 'socially easy' because they are independent of social forces. In reaching this conclusion, Watson refutes what he considers to be a reductionist, instrumentalist understanding that sees law as a mere reflection of social forces. This 'mirror theory of law', which Watson finds in many streams of legal scholarship and in a significant part of sociology, assumes that law is specially tailored for a given society in a definite historical moment and rooted in peculiar local traditions, reflecting the mores, the culture, and the needs of that society. A famous passage in *De l'esprit des lois* epitomizes this belief in a perfect fit between law and society. Baron de

Montesquieu ponders why different nations have different laws and concludes that local laws are deeply embedded in their peculiar religion, climate, geography, commerce, and morals. This diversity would make it *un très grand hasard*, an extraordinary coincidence, if the law designed for one nation could indeed suit another. A wide range of authors with differing ideologies echoed this idea: Savigny's theory of law as living in the common consciousness and the 'spirit' of the people of a nation (*Volksrecht*); the Marxist concept of law as the result of the economic structure of each society that translates the interests of the powerful into domination of the exploited class; Émile Durkheim's index thesis; or Lawrence Friedman's description of American law as fundamentally moulded by economics and society.

In sharp opposition, Watson shows how often legal rules are out of step with the needs and interests of society, and how often law fails to mirror society. In light of the historical evidence he had gathered, he concludes that this perfect fit between law and society hardly exists and that legal evolution is insulated from social change. After all—Watson posits—most legal rules are neutral regarding political and social interests and values, with limited impact on people's lives and on their happiness. Of course, there are significant exceptions. Some legal institutions are deeply embedded in society. The nationalization of the means of production in the Soviet Union gave rise to a new, planned economic system. By stopping treating people as 'things' (*res mancipi*) in Roman law, centuries of slavery were ended. But most rules are technical and apolitical, with only loose ties with culture and society. Legal technicalities about contract and property may be relevant for lawyers, but they are insignificant for society. A rule may order vehicles to drive on the left or on the right, with no substantial difference. In all these cases, we need a rule. Otherwise, no one would know where to drive or who owns what. However, which rule is chosen is quite irrelevant.

A critique

By uncovering the many instances of when law is not the product of local innovation but instead the result of imitation and borrowing, Watson's theory had the merit of putting the accent on the circulation of ideas and institutions as being a major factor of legal change. Also, by offering a dynamic approach to comparison, he contributed to challenging the orthodox taxonomy made up of static legal families and legal systems.

At the same time, his account of legal change has been criticized for being too formalistic and rule-based. The theory of legal transplants and the corollary of their frequency are faulted for ignoring the social and cultural dimensions of law. The ease of legal transplants can be assumed only by confining the analysis to the most manifest levels of the law and to the subtle technicalities of private law, where it is easier to posit a distance between legal rule and society.

Likewise, Watson is accused of seeing legal transplants as taking a unilateral trajectory from one country to another, and of underestimating what happens when laws circulate. The formal transposition of blackletter rules and of 'law in books' can be relatively easy. A foreign text can be taken or imposed on others. But such a mechanical transplant is limited to meaningless words, with little impact on 'law in action'. Interactions and influences in law are never unilateral, as Watson's theory suggests, and the biological metaphor of easy, unilateral legal transplants does not fit a reality where influences are always reciprocal and give rise to complex reactions and transformations.

In response to these criticisms, the focus shifted to how the law is transformed once transplanted, to the importance of local conditions for imported law, and to the process of adaptation of transplanted laws. Passive reception of foreign institutions hardly ever occurs. Once transplanted, rules are inexorably domesticated. In the new context, they acquire a local, autochthonous significance that defies any attempt at uniformity as local agents give new meanings to the imported law following their particular social practices, values, behaviours, traditions, and beliefs, thus transforming the original into something else. This local resistance alters imported laws in ways that are not always foreseeable. It does not prevent the transposition of blackletter rules, but it does trigger an unpredictable series of events. This is what happened for those post-colonial African 'constitutions without constitutionalism' or for the top-down reforms of traditional Hindu family law, which were made nominal by case law.

After all, legal rules and concepts do not travel with their teleology, and this separation between form and substance may render borrowing 'abusive', as in the case of many constitutional reforms described by David Landau and Rosalind Dixon. Doctrines and concepts of liberal democratic constitutionalism promote constitutional institutions and values, from judicial review to constitutional rights. However, in some cases, this legal form is not accompanied by substance. As an example, a constitutional reform that confers the task of preserving the democratic order to a superior court, or the function of guaranteeing the fairness of elections to electoral commissions and anticorruption bodies, may easily have the opposite result if an authoritarian regime takes control of these institutions. Abusive borrowing strategically uses constitutionalism's words and grammar to ends opposite to their original purposes. This is risky not only because it can trigger a 'boomerang effect', subverting rules, doctrines, and concepts into tools to undermine democratic constitutional order, but also because this camouflaged authoritarian attitude behind the façade of liberal democratic forms may generate a concealment effect. Illiberal regimes may replace open intimidation with more subtle forms of coercion, creating a legalistic form of authoritarianism that is more difficult to spot and sanction.

Others argue that while the domestication of foreign law tends to alter the original law, it does not transform it into something familiar to that society. As such, it has an irritant effect. Applying Niklas Luhmann's systems theory in order to illustrate his thesis about 'legal irritants', Gunther Teubner gives the example of the adoption of the continental principle of good faith in British law due to the implementation of European Union law. The continental principle of *bona fides*, meant to counterbalance the strict application of contract law, makes perfect sense in German Rhineland capitalism, based on a business-coordinated market economy. But it stands in stark contrast to the unregulated liberal market economies and the adversarial position of the parties in Common Law countries. Also, such an open-ended general clause is inherently repugnant to British law and unworkable in practice by British courts, with their rule-oriented and concrete style of legal reasoning. According to Teubner, even among not so dissimilar legal systems, such as those of European countries, and even in technical fields of law like contract law, transplanted rules may become 'legal irritants', 'an outside noise which creates wild perturbations'. In short, legal transplants are not only difficult. They are also harmful, since they threaten the genuineness and richness of local cultures and eradicate their diversity.

Legal transplants today

The original meaning of 'legal transplants' was focused on the circulation of formal rules, institutions, and procedures between nation-states, where the circulation of law was seen as following a unilateral trajectory from one country to another: generally, from a 'parent' and 'advanced' to a 'less developed' one. Over time, this narrow meaning broadened to reflect the many different ways laws travel across the contemporary world.

Many scholars have argued that legal transplants do not always move in a North to South, or West to East direction. There are also 'reverse' legal transplants, such as sex-selective abortion in the US, where statutes introducing this kind of limitation routinely refer to India's restrictions, or the adoption of criminal procedure rules in Latin America. The most prominent example of transmission from the Global South is perhaps the widely admired South African constitution, which former US Justice Ruth Bader Ginsburg admitted looking at for guidance, and which many comparativists have studied extensively.

Other cases of reverse legal transplants occur when judges use foreign rules if a specific group is involved, such as the traditional norms applied by Canadian courts in trials with indigenous peoples or the *Sharia* law employed in the UK for trials involving migrants. Multidirectional legal transplants can also be easily spotted when considering laws transplanted by people from a foreign culture, like Muslims or Asian diasporic communities in Europe. Often not incorporated into official law, these minority rules are transplanted by adopting hybridization strategies, giving birth to new forms of normativity, as for the British Muslim law (*angrezi shariat*) or British Hindu law (*angrezi dharma*) narrated by Werner Menski.

While these are all significant examples of the dissemination of law from the Global South to the Global North and from the periphery to the centre, even those who criticize the biased approach of the traditional account concede that the conventional description of a one-way transfer of legal ideas and institutions reflects the *de facto* unidirectionality of legal transplants in practice. This unidirectionality has continued even after the end of the colonial era. In the 1960s and 1970s, the 'law and development' movement tried to transplant laws from 'developed' countries to 'developing' ones to 'modernize' them. A new wave of law reforms took place in the 1990s, producing new constitutions and constitutional frameworks worldwide. As for the reasons behind this circulation, a more benevolent view would be that these legal reforms are a way of strengthening institutions to favour both economic growth and democratic processes or as an attempt by the Global South to gain international legitimacy and attract foreign capital. Critics affirm that these reforms are part of former colonies' domination intentions, with foreign rules designed to facilitate the economic exploitation of weaker countries of the Global South.

Similarly, the account of legal transplants made only by public actors, such as legislators and courts, is placed under scrutiny. In the globalized world, legal transplants are often promoted by private actors, international organizations, non-governmental organizations (NGOs), and networks of lawyers and experts. They take place in a range of informal ways, from private contracting to supply chain policies. In these cases, legal transplants do not always involve a two-stage process from country A to country B. According to the 'IKEA theory of legal transplants', as Günter Frankenberg terms it, an intermediate, additional level often occurs, where rules are decontextualized and mediated in an aterritorial global constitution. Once there, rules are transformed into standardized legal items and labelled as 'best practices', to be bought and sold worldwide. This standardization of law converts rules into a global reservoir of marketable commodities available for law reforms at the world's four corners, providing good enough legal solutions at a reasonable price for countries which cannot afford to formulate tailor-made reforms.

Chapter 3
Legal traditions

Legal traditions have (partially) replaced legal families in current scholarship, as they emphasize the evolving nature of the law, its fluidity and hybridity, overcoming the rigid boundaries set by the taxonomic project. They are more appropriate for capturing the experiences of the entire world, thus reducing the shortcomings of previous classifications.

Traditions show the diachronic, historical, and cultural magnitudes of the law, since they rely upon constant reflexive processes, through looping or feedback. Time plays a role in the construction of traditions, with past practices being a necessary reference. Each tradition embeds distinctly rooted, historically determined understandings of the role of law in a society, its organization as a system, and the way it is elaborated, interpreted, and learnt, as John Henry Merryman would put it. Then, how many years, or centuries, are required to establish a tradition? This question remains unanswered but, since time is necessary in any case to appreciate the novelty, originality, and diffusion of a 'new' tradition, immediate traditions would be impossible to grasp.

In comparative scholarship, H. Patrick Glenn has elaborated a very well-known classification of the 'legal traditions of the world', providing a template based on seven categories: Chthonic (or folk), Talmudic, Civil Law, Islamic, Common Law, Hindu, and Confucian. Partially departing from this classification, the following sections of the chapter offer a synthetic and syncretic overview of the major legal traditions.

This chapter maps the traditions through four categories: oral (Chthonic; African); religious (Talmudic; Islamic); traditions emphasizing duties (Hindu; Confucian); and Western traditions recognizing state authority as the source of the system (Common; Civil). For each, the most characteristic feature is highlighted, while recognizing that they are not homogeneous from a material standpoint. More detailed, substantial issues are to be found within the corresponding descriptions. The chthonic tradition is addressed first, as it presents more geographical and historical transversality.

Western traditions are analysed in the final part of the chapter since they mainly correspond to the legal families introduced in Chapter 2 which were identically named. Two distinct understandings of positive law (*ius positum*; decided by individuals and provided with authority by the state) emerged as fixed by different entities within the legal system. Civil Law jurisdictions opted for codifying their law, while Common Law countries developed the mechanism of 'binding precedent', linked to that of *stare decisis*, in order to provide consistency to the legal system. Almost at the same time, in the US these mechanisms coexisted, with both state codifications and binding precedents.

A 'Western legal tradition' has been identified, building upon common features among which are: the distinction between legal and non-legal institutions; the existence of professionals dealing with the administration of legal institutions; the establishment of dedicated training and educational paths to exercise such professions; the inclusion of scholarship within the study of law; the conception of law as an integrated system; the belief in a logical development of law; and the existence of diverse systems in the same community, according to Harold J. Berman. These features partially correspond to those of the 'rule of professional law' elaborated by Ugo Mattei and mentioned in Chapter 2. Legal pluralism depended on the separation between secular (royal, urban, feudal) and ecclesiastical realms, since the members of the communities could be subject to ecclesiastical norms with respect to family while being normally ruled by secular norms and, therefore, subject to the king's or lord's court. Members of the church could also be brought in front of secular jurisdictions in certain matters. The complexity of coexisting different systems within one order contributed to the sophistication of Western legal thought.

Western legal arrangements have long been considered the benchmark of development and efficiency in comparative scholarship. The predominance of Western-based categories is due to the fact that Western scholars have been trying to achieve these formal definitions for more than a century through comparative legal studies. In contrast, other traditions have been far less concerned with taxonomies and strictly legal assessments of their roots. Additionally, it is connected to the relationship between the law and the state in Western-like systems, and to the role of modern states when dealing with different traditions. Several examples mentioned in the chapter demonstrate the complex relationship between state law and oral or religious traditions. Such 'prejudice' is slowly being overcome. The shift from legal families to traditions represents a step in that direction.

Oral traditions: Informality and community

Chthonic tradition. The law is an element inherent to any community, including those in which it mixes with customs and religious beliefs without formalized deliberation by established institutions. From a Western, external perspective, such communities were labelled as simply 'folk'. Trying to analyse them from an internal perspective, Glenn names them 'chthonic'.

This tradition is linked to the cosmos and has been applied particularly to indigenous groups living in close harmony with the earth, as pointed out by Edward Goldsmith, in parts of Latin America, Africa, and the South Pacific. No specific timeframe can be applied to this tradition (unlike the others) since time is not perceived as a flowing stream, but as a circular, immanent phenomenon. Moreover, no proper evolution is known; this tradition is mainly concerned with the conservation of the sacred value of the world.

The plethora of cases and experiences covered by this tradition does not represent an impediment to finding commonalities. The chthonic tradition is primarily based on oral norms, experience, and memory, without any set point of origin or revelation. Orality implies the rejection of excessive formality and details as well as the involvement of the entire community (relatively small, in principle) in learning relevant information. Institutional settings appear to be less complex, often relying on a council of elders and sometimes on the role of a recognized chief. Basic legal institutions, such as family arrangements, are based on informal agreements and consensual decisions, and potential disputes are also settled through informal mechanisms.

There are no proper individual rights within any legal domain. Even criminal issues are conceived as a responsibility of the group and are managed with a focus on restoring the community rather than on the punishment of the guilty party. Significantly, the synergic relationship between people and land constitutes a further fundamental element of this tradition, with shared enjoyment, customary land, and common (not individually owned) property.

Openness and informality make the chthonic tradition particularly porous and prone to contamination, as it is little equipped to counteract external impositions and influence. The progressive spread of states all over the world has led to a necessary coexistence between this tradition and 'others', in particular, with Western models in colonized territories, with temporary (Asian and African) or permanent (Australasian and American) settlements. Thus, the distinction of the 'colonial', 'post-colonial', and/or 'neo-colonial' is not an easy task, as Upendra Baxi underlines.

Chthonic worldviews and cosmogonies still exist and may differ from those of nation-states. The indigenous *buen vivir*, which entails collective arrangements in harmony with nature, based on solidarity and far away from capitalism and the Western conception of economic development, represents an example. It was integrated in the Bolivian constitution as a plural concept deriving from several chthonic traditions, while the Ecuadorian constitution explicitly refers to the homologous *sumak kawsay* of the Quechua community. It leads the state to pursue integrated and sustainable actions in economic, political, and environmental choices in order to establish a supportive economy, participation, promotion of interculturalism, and the preservation of natural resources.

Africa provides relevant examples as well in this respect. In Sierra Leone, traditionally, each person understands their worth in the nurturing of linkages with other people and not in their individuality. Thinking of others first and being connected, rather than being autonomous as in individualistic societies, is core to societal arrangements, which differ from the more competitive and individualistic Western elaborations. The traditional Zulu concept of *Ubuntu* is shared by many tribal societies (with different denominations) and presents similar aspects to *buen vivir*, as it entails social bonds based on human solidarity for the fulfilment of each life. It was present in the constituent debates of South Africa and it has been included in case law quite extensively.

Arrangements between non-chthonic state law and chthonic law are not always easy. States have had to accept legal arrangements of chthonic communities, as was the case for aboriginal adoption law in the Canadian case *Casimel v. Insurance Corporation of British Columbia*, 1993. The regulation of collective land use/property is an excellent example, as in some countries the territory subject to similar forms of property represents up to a third (such as Colombia) of the whole. Contemporary constitutions (e.g., Brazil 1988; Colombia 1991; Ecuador 2008; Bolivia 2009), legislation, and national and international jurisdictions have had to tackle this conception of property and accommodate it within different standards. For example, New Zealand established a specialized Māori Land Court to promote the retention and use of land, while fostering its occupation, use, and development; or the Canadian Supreme Court has managed the concept of 'community usufruct over land' over time since the 19th century (*St. Catharines Milling and Lumber Co. v. The Queen*, 1887), explaining that such an aboriginal title is automatically extinguished. The Mexican Supreme Court has dealt with cases concerning the exploitation of indigenous lands (for instance with respect to mining concessions). At the international level, both the Inter-American Commission and the Inter-American Court of Human Rights have decided upon communal ownership in cases like *Comunidad Mayagna (Sumo) Awas Tingni v. Nicaragua* (2001) or *Comunidad Indígena Sawhoyamaxa v. Paraguay* (2006). They have stated that distinct, more ancestral forms of dominion and possession of land are worth protecting under the American Convention, and have recognized that they derive from culture, customs, and intrinsic beliefs connected to the existence of the affected communities. There is, in fact, both a material and a cultural connection with the land, which leads to respect and preservation of natural elements, such as animals and the environment.

African traditions. African legal tradition, or *rectius* traditions, have long represented the most neglected orders in comparative scholarship, in spite of increasing interest from scholars, as well as those which more clearly suffer from the bias of the Western conception of law when combined with colonial history. There is a partial overlap with chthonic features as they mainly rely on oral transmission of customary rules, with a plurality of interpreters and, therefore, a communal elaboration. From a Western perspective, colonial linkages have determined classifications based on previously belonging to an area of influence. Excluding a few hybrids, former French, Spanish, Portuguese, and Italian colonies were attached to the Civil Law tradition; and the former British colonies were assigned to Common Law, while Northern Africa was separated due to the relevant Islamic legal component.

Nevertheless, African traditions are composed of different legal layers, and some of them date back to the pre-colonial period. Distinct societal arrangements existed before colonization, which either relied on or lacked a structure around leadership (such as for the Pygmies). Magical and supernatural beliefs played a role as well in shaping the rules of coexistence along with the impact of different religions (Muslim or Christian in Sub-Saharan Africa) through waves of migration and conquest. In between religion, magical faith, and law, the role of ancestors and the elderly should be placed in order to understand the collective dimension of families' and groups' legal arrangements. African traditional law often relies as well on communal ownership of the land which was, and is, challenged by individual ownership under Western standards.

The approach of Western colonizers, who thought of themselves as 'civilized people', was to enlighten and reform local customs and laws. The waves of colonization were sources of legal pluralism in the continent, reinforcing the distinct legal-historical narratives of Southern Africa, tropical Africa, and Madagascar. The imposition of Roman-Dutch law in the 17th century and the subsequent British Occupation (1795) determined the hybrid nature of Cape colonial law, which was added to the legal systems of Southern African territories and Boer Republics. Tropical Africa relies mainly upon customary law, which has over time been combined with Western paradigms; while Madagascar, a former French colony, soon became an independent kingdom (1824), recovering and codifying its customary norms but keeping elements of French law. Hybrid systems are no exception. Former British colonies, such as Zambia, Malawi, and Zimbabwe, have in their legal construction customary law and Common Law; while Somalia combines customary law and Islamic elements.

Religious traditions: divine revelations in need of interpretation

Talmudic tradition. The Talmudic tradition is characterized by the aim of regulating all aspects of life, designing an all-encompassing code of conduct for the members of the community. Geographically, it is identified with Israel, although it represents a body of norms applicable to Jews, independent of where they live.

The legal basis is the *Torah* ('Teaching'), namely, the first five books—Pentateuch—of the Bible. Therefore, this tradition has a religious basis. The divine nature of the law forbids amendments, but contextually entails interpretation and application, which are required of humans by God.

Along with the *Torah*, the oral *Torah* is composed of additional rules and interpretations which are valued as prescriptive. Two layers of oral *Torah* have successively been elaborated, earlier the *Mishnah*, which represents the first relevant compilation of commentaries of the teachers over the 1st and 2nd centuries CE. When the persecution of the Jewish communities made it likely that this tradition would be lost, it was written down, made public, and studied by subsequent generations of rabbis in Israel. The second layer is represented by the so-called *Gemara*, a rabbinic, metacommentary examination of the *Mishnah*. Taken together, the *Mishnah* and the *Gemara* lead to the *Talmud* ('Instruction'), i.e., the main text of Rabbinic Judaism and the primary source of Jewish religious law and theology. A plurality of issues is addressed by the *Talmud*, which contains two main categories of statements: law and practice, 'the way to walk' (*halakha*) and non-legally binding aspects related to ethics, history, culture, etc. (*aggadah*). For instance, the *shabbat* is a day that must be dedicated to rest and devotion. Therefore, several activities are not allowed, such as doing business, shopping, driving vehicles, using the telephone, or turning on/off electric devices and tools.

Interpretation plays a major role in this tradition, since the law was designed to be understood, interpreted, and conveyed by human beings. This mechanism leads to potentially conflicting interpretations, because when they are delivered in good faith and intellectual honesty, they are contextually correct as they reflect a holistic appraisal of the law and do not lack objectivity. The overall creation of the law is a joint enterprise with different contextual interpretations provided by several authors, although in practice, there is a need for univocal solutions. Therefore, rabbis within their jurisdiction are entitled to decide on the application of the 613 commandments addressed to Jewish people and the seven commandments for the 'children of Noah', i.e., for the whole of humanity (the last one regards establishing courts of justice). Procedurally, higher decisions must be respected and, in cases where there are none, the rabbi must decide with piety, honesty, and decency, according to colleagues' previous decisions, if at all possible. There is continuity through time and collective interpretation, since the great rabbis from previous generations are taken into consideration by contemporary rabbis and scholars who 'modernize' the rules in light of the corresponding community's understanding.

Talmudic Law applicability, by tradition, depended on the individual affected more than on geography. From the Middle Ages, its precepts were applied in family and commercial disputes (in Spain, in criminal law as well). Together with family law, which is a key component of personal laws, trade/commercial law has always been a particularly relevant domain in Talmudic Law. Still, it absorbed institutions derived from Islamic Law in order to allow for easier commercial exchanges with Muslim counterparts.

Also outside Israel, tradition required the establishment of a rabbinical court in each community with a chief rabbi assisted by associate judges who could require the litigants to appear before them. Such obligations have been diluted over time, and often the parties obtain an exemption to file a case before ordinary courts, since formally referring to non-rabbinical courts would imply idolatry. Nevertheless, no violation of Jewish norms can be excused because it represents an obligation under the local legal system, one example being that voting on Saturdays violates the *shabbat*.

Islamic tradition. Islamic Law also embraces the entire existence of the individual and aims at one major goal, namely the welfare of the people. The 'Way of God and the Pathway of Goodness' (the *Sharia*) is revealed through various evidence and indicators, the first of which are the textual sources. Nevertheless, not all rules can be inferred from the text, since customs, reason, and intuition contribute as well, providing adaptability of the law over time.

This tradition, as well as having evolved over the centuries, geographically concerns Central and South-East Asia (with the exception of Buddhist countries, such as Thailand, Myanmar, or Cambodia), as well as African countries, such as Egypt, Tunisia, Sudan, and Somalia. Islamic jurisprudence in classical terms began in the period from the 8th to the 9th centuries and continued to be relevant until the mid-19th century, according to Colin Imber. Legal books from the Ottoman Empire started to be adopted in the 15th century and culminated in the Land Code of 1858, including *Sharia* principles in sporadic cases. Interpretation through legal scholarship (*Fiqh*) was realized by each school (*Madhhab*). There were different schools for the distinct branches of Islam. Within the same school, plurality of orientations was accepted, and the corresponding members delivered persuasive opinions, any of which could then become predominant and be applied in concrete cases. Potentially different interpretations could be legitimate if they were elaborated with due diligence.

Islamic Law, as such, reflects the characters used in Arabic, which only puts consonants in writing, giving rise to heated philological discussions. The reasoning differs from Western legal thought, as in the Talmudic tradition. It was developed in terms of probabilities and through the application of categories such as 'free' or 'recommended' (conduct), 'reprehensible', 'obligatory', or 'forbidden'.

Like the Talmudic tradition, the foundation of the law is divine and is to be found within a revelation—in this case from God to Muhammad—over more than two decades, i.e., the *Qur'an* ('Recitation'). Few specific obligations can be found in the text and a literalist interpretation would hardly stand. Therefore, Muslim scholars of *Fiqh* have developed sophisticated hermeneutics to infer the legal implications of the *Qur'an* and have addressed the 'occasions of revelation' to contextualize the teachings, distinguish between temporal and sacred actions, and detail the time and cause of portions of the *Qur'an*.

The second divine source is found in the so-called *Sunnah*, which is composed of practices and traditions collected in *hadith* (teachings, sayings, silent permissions, and disapprovals, as well as stories mainly from Muhammad's life), establishing a model for Muslims to follow. Alongside the monotheistic beliefs, other more mundane aspects are addressed, such as the necessity to be charitable and to be gentle or well-mannered when invited. Different teachings are recognized depending on the streams of Islam, and they are classified according to their authoritative and epistemic significance as well as the number of narrators reporting them. The consistency and linearity of narrators greatly contributes to the recognition of the norm.

In this tradition, analogy and deductive reasoning play a major role. Analogical reasoning (*qiyas*) is applied to deduce legal principles and norms from the divine sources. Not long after Muhammad passed away, this exegetical tool became relevant for applying the *Qur'an* and the *Sunnah* to newly conquered territories which presented distinct conditions, either by establishing new solutions or by legitimizing previous ones. For example, the prohibition of selling and buying goods after the last call for prayers on Fridays has been extended analogically so as to also forbid other transactions and activities. Furthermore, the prohibition of smoking has been deduced from different obligations, namely, the prohibition on harming one's body and the prohibition on consuming alcoholic beverages because there are more negative effects than positive ones.

Since the role of interpreters is fundamental, the consensus among jurists (*Ijma*) also amounts to a binding source for subsequent generations. In fact, this term identifies a consensus achieved in the near or remote past that is vested in authority. For instance, concerning the sale of a good under the condition of being absent of defects, there was consensus that whoever sold a slave or an animal could not be held responsible for the defect unless he knew about it in advance and hid it. Several guiding principles can be employed in interpretation to enhance predictability and stability. Nora Zeineddine recalls the presumption of continuity, the respect for precedents, the application of customs, the use of equity, and the pursuit of public interest.

Traditions of duties (before rights)

Hindu tradition. One of the most ancient traditions is the Hindu one, spanning over three millennia, and also one of the most widely spread geographically. Hindu Law does not only refer territorially to India itself, it also represents a layer of complex legal systems, e.g., of Pakistan, Malaysia, Nepal, Singapore,

Myanmar; as well as African countries, such as Kenya or Uganda; and South American countries, such as Surinam. In spite of its reach, this tradition has often been overlooked in appraisals of comparative law due to reasons linked to language (classical sources have Sanskrit-based foundations) or reduced utility due to the prevalence of Common Law and codified sources in contemporary India for practising lawyers. Its evolution can be divided into four phases, described by Werner Menski as follows: from 'the macrocosmic universal Order (*rita*) of the Vedic system to the microcosmic self-controlled order (*dharma*) of classical Hindu Law proper, and the deterrence-based stage of punishment (*danda*) and more or less formal dispute processing (*vyavahāra*) in the late classical and postclassical system'.

This is not a full-fledged religious tradition, but rather a 'religiously inspired' one, with its basis being Hindu thought in which sources of law are elaborated *ad hoc*. Hinduism and Hindu Law do not necessarily coincide, and Hinduism does not oblige its adherents to be subject to a divinity; there is no personalization in a totally theistic manner.

Interpretation of norms is paramount in this tradition, as it is for Talmudic and Islamic Law, as change of the primary sources is not permitted. The conceptual foundation is *dharma*, which represents the all-encompassing duty to do the right thing at the right time and is composed of norms, behaviours, moral actions, and ethical attitudes. Individuals have to follow them in order to lead a harmonious existence, depending on their role in society, their profession, family position, and caste. The term also embeds civil, commercial, and criminal institutions. It is connected to *karma*, that is, the belief in the impact of previous actions on a person's future, which affects the understating of existence within society and across generations. Cultures and customs are crucial in the construction of normativity, and Hindu Law encompasses a plurality of legal systems, similarly to Islamic Law but not as much as African Law.

The Vedas (*Rigveda*, *Yajurveda*, *Samaveda*, and *Atharvaveda*) represented the basic religious texts, which entail a sort of revelation without giving much emphasis to the messenger or to the author. They were basically ritual manuals. Brahmans were entitled to teach the Vedas and they initially did so orally. Vedic law covered a period approximately from the year 1500 BCE to the 5th century BCE. Over time, explanations were written in the *Smriti* ('what is remembered'), a corpus of various texts which represent derivative and auxiliary written sources, whose authority also relies on the ancient, orally transmitted Vedic literature called *Shruti* ('what is heard'). The copious and diverse metaliterature, which added up to existing traditions and customs, can be divided into *Dharmasutra* and *Dharmashastra* texts.

Only four out of the approximately twenty *sutras* that have been accounted for have survived into the modern era. They were composed in an aphoristic style and left much room for interpretation. This tradition ended around the start of the common era and was followed up by the emergence of the *Dharmashastras*, written in octosyllables covering rituals, religious observance, expiation, as well as conducts related to family, property, and succession law in particular. Three *shastras* have special relevance, and above all the Laws of Manu, the most ancient dating back most likely to the 1st century BCE, had to prevail in cases of conflict. The later commentaries and digests built upon these sources, representing further exegetical layers of the foundational norms. Formal schools arose around the 7th century, which nonetheless valued and embraced local traditions, reducing conflicts. Therefore, in contrast to the Islamic tradition, the idea of law-making by sages is not so paramount in this tradition.

Since tolerance and pluralism are at the core of the understanding of law and society, it did not counter other traditions with force. In India, for instance, hybridity derived from the significant impact of Islamic Law first and colonial domination later. British colonizers wished to transform Hindu and Islamic norms into personal statutes. Hindu sources were translated into English and recognized as the law of the Hindu population. However, the translations did not manage to convey the cultural, more than the legal, dimension of these documents. Nevertheless, when the Indian subcontinent was ruled by the United Kingdom, the pervasiveness of the Common Law was more subtle than in other geographical areas, and it particularly relied on the role of judges and the incorporation of the binding precedent of British Common Law.

Confucian tradition. Chinese law has been explored relatively often in comparative scholarship, at first within the 'systems of the Far East' as was explained in Chapter 2. China became a centralized kingdom in the 3rd century BCE (lasting until 1911, and ending with the Qing dynasty) and its construction was connected to the Confucian conception of the law. Norms deriving from authority, named *fa*, made up the core of the system and were addressed to the administration, more than to the people. The major fields were criminal and administrative law and focused on sanctions. Their codes characterized state law until the 20th century, being admired in Europe and translated into several languages.

The rest of the legal system was dominated by the so-called *li*, customary, traditional, socially embedded norms responding to the basic conception of the society's and the group's organization. It relies upon the community's adhesion to the values and encompasses habits, rituals, and morals. It is composed of duties and obligations towards the society or its fractions. This emerges clearly in business relationships which are intended to be fluid and aim at mutual satisfaction. Therefore, *li* has an extremely relational foundation, as it views the individuals' fulfilment as a component of their role within a group, be it the family or a professional community. Individual rights were not core elements in the Chinese tradition (nor in the subsequent socialist or communist laws, which found a fruitful philosophical substrate in this duty-oriented mentality), in spite of the assumption of the natural goodness of mankind. The perspective adopted to explain relations was that of the debtor, and not that of the holder of the corresponding right.

Social harmony is a key element of Confucianism, which leads to informal normativity with little emphasis on the individual but rather on punishment and obligations. This harmony is profoundly related to intergenerational equilibria, which reinforce the role of the elderly in families, as well as in societal and professional organizations. The impact of religion is relatively small, be it Buddhism, Taoism, or other influential beliefs.

Different layers are also present in contemporary Chinese law, determined by historical events. Europeanization was a key element of the codes adopted in the early 19th century by the nationalist Republic of Jiang Jieshi, which were totally overcome after the proclamation of the Popular Republic in 1949. Later on, the inclusion of Western legal models in the organization of the judiciary or legal professions, among others, has hardly taken root in the societal understanding of reciprocal interaction.

The Confucian tradition has influenced East Asia, Korea, and Japan. In the latter, *li* basically corresponds to *giri*, which is a sort of obligation to gratitude or loyalty. Japan was also influenced by the codification of German private law (and at the time therefore included in the Civil Law area), which overlapped informal normativity. US law was influential after the Second World War in a few domains, such as constitutional law. Also other countries, such as modern Indonesia and Malaysia, were shaped by Chinese law, alongside the significant influence of Islamic Law. Malaysia itself, Hong Kong, and Singapore combine this root with a Common Law organization of legal professions.

Western traditions: the seal of state authority

Common Law tradition. The Common Law tradition dates back to the 11th century, when the Normans conquered England (1066) and wished to achieve stability and peace in the new territories where norms already existed. They believed that the instrument for the achievement of peace was a loyal judiciary. In their need for permanent judicial officers, priests were chosen as they were literate and had legal notions in their background deriving from canon law (norms regulating Christianity and emanating from religious authority). Nevertheless, the new justice system could not be completely exogenous. Therefore, juries composed of locals were established to act as the 'law-finders', applying traditional norms to each case. Common Law embraced the logic of the existing society to avoid rejection and non-recognition.

As was explained in Chapter 2, the original Common Law relied upon procedural norms more than substantive norms. The latter were basically local rules brought to the judge by jury members. The procedure was based on the so-called 'writs' or 'forms of action', which initiated a particular procedure or remedy. The writs consisted of instructions from the crown to a royal officer stating what he should do to investigate the case. This implied that justice emanated from the crown, which also had control of what legal situations were protected. Since this society was mostly agriculture based, the writs covered mainly land-ownership-related issues, debt, and covenant (for commercial law) as well as trespass. Trespass was a comprehensive form of action, labelled by the well-known English historian Frederic William Maitland as the 'fertile mother of actions', from which trespass for assault and battery, trespass to chattels, trespass to land, and other actions derived as 'living things', as forms of action were in the beginning.

Family law was not addressed because it was regulated by traditions and, where necessary, by religious norms. Interestingly, it was a law of relations and mutual obligations, without the prominent role of the individual, which entered into Western thought later, during the Enlightenment.

The decision on the merits was allotted to the members of the juries who, unlike judges, were usually illiterate and performed other occupations. Necessarily, therefore, argument and proof were oral. The judge deliberated on whether the precise case was consistent with the scope of the writ invoked and, if this was the case, he was in charge of the correct application of procedure. Since the selected writ could not be changed afterwards, the plaintiff knew from the start on what grounds he would win or lose.

There was just a first instance. The mechanism was based on the idea of 'peer judgement', and peers could not be mistaken. No binding precedent existed, unlike in subsequent developments and the widespread concept of Common Law.

The remedies were fifty in the 13th century, when they began to be enumerated, and their number increased by half in the 19th century. They proved to be extremely rigid mechanisms which exclusively covered a few situations and did not provide judges with the necessary margin of interpretation to protect new legal demands.

The first response of Common Law came from the crown and was the transformation of the Chancery into a proper tribunal around the 15th century, exerting jurisdiction over those cases not covered by the writs and elaborating complementary norms. This case law—equity jurisprudence—was unified with Common Law through the major reforms of the 19th century. In particular, the fixed writs were replaced by 'open courts', to which people could submit cases, expecting the courts to apply the law. The role of judges changed radically, as they were supposed to decide on the merits. Unlike juries, they could be found to be mistaken and their decisions could be taken to the Court of Appeal and finally the House of Lords. Juries were then relegated to deciding exclusively only on certain matters.

Thus, the paramount idea characterizing modern Common Law, namely judicial law-making with binding value, arose relatively recently, with the need for a systematic ordering of judgements to ensure legal certainty. The obligation to follow previous decisions, in fact, implies that each judgement does not merely create rules for the specific case, but fixes objective law. This mechanism does not apply to the entire judgement, and not all judgements can serve as precedents. Only the legal foundation or reason (*ratio decidendi*) of a specific case sets a precedent, with the exclusion of the other additional, factual elements (*obiter dicta*); and ordinarily vertical precedents are binding, i.e., judgements adopted by higher courts.

The system of precedent entails a certain degree of rigidity. Therefore, two basic tools to avoid following a precedent are in place, namely (a) 'distinguishing' when a subsequent judge considers that the case before him differs significantly from the previous one and, therefore, establishes a new precedent for the situation under his judgement; and (b) 'overruling', when the precedent is replaced by a novel *ratio decidendi*, more consistent with the current legal/social situation, by a court that is entitled to oblige the others. Generally, the obligation of an inferior court to follow the case law of a higher court is taken to be stricter than the obligation of the higher court to respect its own precedent. Since 1966, the House of Lords, as well as the UK Supreme Court now, can overrule its previous decisions (the US Supreme Court does not appear to be bound by a similar obligation).

The Common Law tradition has spread throughout the world via historical and colonial paths. English law was already applied in Ireland in the 12th century and the members of the Commonwealth have maintained the basic structures of Common

Law. Canada, Australia, and New Zealand still have several elements of this tradition, although over time they have mixed them with Civil Law models. South Africa and India are also included in this group, but with the peculiarities and mixtures already mentioned in this chapter. The United States of America represents the other major model of Common Law. It has constructed its base with components which do not exist in the UK, such as a rigid constitution, federalism, and constitutional adjudication. It has influenced Central and South America and is a reference within the tradition.

Civil Law tradition. Differently from Common Law, where judgements are primary sources of law and their logical organization is essential for constructing the legal order, the other major Western legal tradition allots primary law-making to the legislature. This is certainly true for what the classification into families used to call modern Civil Law, meaning the period after the codification of the 19th century. The Roman period (from the Twelve Tables of the 5th century BCE) allotted relevance to the advice provided by jurisconsults, particularly the glosses of the commentators of the first universities (especially Bologna in 1088; Figure 4) on the compilation of Roman law ordered by Justinian I in the 6th century. As mentioned in Chapter 2, their interpretations gave rise to a new substantive law, the *ius commune*, which ruled continental Europe between the 11th and the 19th century. Canon law also developed here alongside Roman law and contributed to overcoming chthonic legal arrangements over time.

Unlike taxonomies elaborated under the 'families' umbrella, taking Civil Law into account diachronically allows for an understanding of how chthonic arrangements gave rise to this tradition. No clear-cut distinction between the Roman and the modern phases is seen, but rather an evolution. The Roman formulary procedure to have one's case heard—which did not differ very much from the original Common Law—was based on

4. Portrait of Irnerius, the renowned medieval jurist who founded the School of Glossators in Bologna.

two stages: first, a screening by the *praetor*, who was in charge of passing an edict listing the cases to be heard, and then the decision by the judge. Jurisconsults' opinions covered first family law, expanding to property and contracts, and gaining prestige and respect for being able to govern complex human relationships.

The philosophical belief in the rationality of the law and the need for written sources, along with the emergence of nation-states, led to one of the major features of the tradition, namely the adoption of codes. Nevertheless, this phenomenon followed more ancient features such as the need for resident judges in charge of procedure and the prestige given to law professors.

Roman law had a very low level of abstraction and referred to daily common events and objects. In contrast, current Civil Law legislation is general and abstract to enable its application to different concrete situations. The Enlightenment had an impact on this style, as well as on the rise of individual rights, replacing the relational and obligational structure of Roman law. The law became a tool of reason, and a legal solution can be logically inferred from general provisions contained in the formal written sources provided by public authorities. Therefore, one additional feature of the Civil Law tradition is the construction of legal orders as systems.

Understood in this way, those codes, which were the focus of taxonomic studies, became a way to follow the diffusion of this model more than being the main intrinsic feature of the tradition. The most prominent was the French Civil Code (1804), which represented a novel way of organizing the regulation of a branch of law. The term was already adopted in Roman law before the Bolognese legal school and was then chosen by revolutionaries in France to define their legal *corpus*. It identifies a comprehensive statutory body of law, capable of regulating all possible situations within a branch of law, passed by legislatures and made public for citizens. The French codification was an extremely successful model and was subject to widespread diffusion, not only in Italy, Switzerland, Belgium, and the Netherlands, but also widely imitated in Latin America and Africa.

The corresponding German code on civil/private law, coming into force in 1900 (Bürgerliches Gesetzbuch; BGB), also spread outside German borders and influenced legal systems in Eastern Europe (e.g., Yugoslavia and Hungary), Latin America (e.g., Brazil and Peru), and even Asia (e.g., China and Japan). Its influence overlapped with the French one in other countries, such as Switzerland or Italy. Overall, continental European and Latin American systems provide the major examples of Civil Law legal systems, as the latter have codes inspired by European models and their circulation is favoured by language, especially with respect to Spain or Portugal. Language is, in fact, a crucial element for fostering the diffusion of models, as well as in deciding their success or failure. The spread of English Common Law to English-speaking countries also proves this point (see Chapter 6).

Codes have been divided, progressively, into substantive matters (civil, criminal, administrative law, etc.) and procedural matters (civil procedure, criminal procedure, etc.), preserving the idea that comprehensive and constantly updated legal codes could contain all matters potentially submittable to a court, the applicable procedure, and the corresponding sanctions. If the law-making power is allotted to the legislature, therefore, the role of the judiciary differs from that given to them in Common Law. They apply the norms decided by political authorities to concrete cases. Their reasoning is labelled as deductive because they interpret the abstract and general clauses contained in codes and pieces of legislation to decide on the merits of the cases. By contrast, the reasoning of Common Law is defined as inductive, because a decision delivered in a given real case will become the basis from which general rules (the *rationes decidendi* of the precedents) are inferred. Civil Law pursues a more clear-cut separation of powers, preventing judges from law-making. This explains why judges can be elected in Common Law depending on the actual post, since they are the ones deciding the 'rules of the game' for the community. In Civil Law countries they are normally selected through public examinations. In other words, popular legitimacy through elections (or even indirectly through appointment by political authorities) makes sense for judges entitled to law-making, but not for technical bodies enforcing parliamentary decisions.

Traditions, time, and geography

History has affected all traditions. The development of the Western tradition has been determined, according to Harold J. Berman, by different revolutionary moments (the Russian, the French, the American, or the Protestant

Reformation), which have led to new societal and economic arrangements as well as novel legal structures and foundations. Civil Law thinking was particularly influenced by the Enlightenment. Moreover, African, Latin American, and Asian systems have been affected to different extents by phenomena of colonization and decolonization. In its colonies, France pursued the 'civilization' of territories through legal uniformity, while British and Spanish colonizers partially involved locals in the administration.

Most of the world's population lives in Asia, where European colonization was a transitory event, similar to the Middle East and Africa. The widest part of the world is subject to non-Western legal orders in which the traditional sources do not emanate directly from the state (as is the case for Talmudic, Islamic, and Hindu traditions, and, even more so, the oral ones).

From this perspective, traditions incorporate religious and indigenous legal arrangements into the methodology of comparative law, assessing their nature, the underlying justifications, the concept of change, and their mutual relationships. Therefore, they grasp non-state forms of legal normativity while earlier taxonomies excluded from their scope norms that did not respond to 'Westphalian' criteria. Asia and Africa have different conceptions of territory and boundaries that do not necessarily reflect the fixity of state borders. Chthonic legal arrangements are totally disconnected from state authority as such, while Talmudic and Islamic Law are attached to specific communities, being laws of individuals rather than states; and Hindu Law situates itself somewhere in between. Personal statutes have, therefore, particular relevance in non-Western systems, as they were already recognized in the Ottoman Empire as the prerogative of people belonging to a certain religious group.

History is essential to understand traditions, and so is geography. The Islamic, Hindu, or Talmudic traditions are often labelled as

Asian, while Common Law and Civil Law are correctly labelled as Western, but there are overlaps, and the geographical indication only applies to the majority of the cases without being able to confine all relevant legal orders within one continent or area. In this respect, colonizations and migrations are key phenomena, which have moulded legal geography over time. If the former implied the imposition of Western standards in other parts of the world, the latter will determine a constant reshaping of place as people move between different origins and destinations, bringing their legal background with them and interacting with various local traditions.

Still, a combination of history and geography helps situate the legal roots of institutional and societal arrangements. Contemporary settings are the outcome of centuries of circulation of models, mutual influences, conquests, cultural dominance, or practical aims. The colonial heritage has affected African, Latin American, and Asian systems. In Asia, hybridity is certainly a major feature of the continent. This is graphically explained through the image of Asian 'legal circles', recently recalled by Janos Jany, in which there is a dominant legal culture (such as the Chinese, for instance) and several satellite cultures which have drawn inspiration from this (such as in Korea or Vietnam). By contrast, even in the Middle Ages, Central Asia was mainly devoted to Islamic Law and still is. The diffusion of this tradition was connected to economic factors and so it spread as well to the archipelago of South-East Asia, which was mostly not under the influence of the Chinese or Hindu models. Of course, the expansion of a consolidated tradition did not necessarily lead to a successful adoption of the dominant model in the territories under its influence. Returning to the Chinese example, Japan received the influence of Confucian Law and legal thinking, but it did not fully embrace it.

Generally speaking, before Western colonization, Asian legal circles maintained stable boundaries and did not undergo major phenomena of diffusion, particularly between the 'dominant' systems. Chinese and Hindu Law proved to be particularly immune from mutual influence in spite of the multiple commercial exchanges and trade. Satellite legal systems were more inclined to receive and mix other models, but still, it was a rare phenomenon and even led to reactions by the dominant legal system and its institutions. An example is the Buddhist influence on Japanese law. Buddhism profoundly influenced Cambodia, Laos, Sri Lanka, Bhutan, and Vietnam as well.

Within the continent, the relationship between Islamic and Hindu Law is significant to grasp the overlap and coexistence of traditions. They have experienced much internal development, including the recent, more intense influence from Western laws. As Menski puts it, these two traditions also present similarities in the tensions between 'the religious' and 'the secular'.

Further transversal issues

No clear-cut distinction between traditions ultimately stands—even between Common Law and Civil Law. Mutual influence and convergence are known. Civil Law courts rely on previous judgements of higher jurisdictions to follow prestigious precedents and/or reduce the grounds for their judgement to be reversed on appeal. Common Law countries, like the US, at both federal and state level, have an increasing body of statutory law alongside case law. In addition, a few countries show patterns of evolution between the Common Law and the Civil Law traditions, such as the Scandinavian countries or the state of Louisiana in the US, similarly to the province of Quebec in Canada, where private/civil law is regulated under the standards of the Civilian tradition and the rest of the legal system is based on Canadian Common Law. Likewise, South Africa combines Roman-Dutch law and English law, which was applied in the Cape Colony during the colonial period. In Israel, historical layers deriving from the British Mandate in Palestine favoured the spread of English

Common Law, maintained after 1948 and then combined with elements coming from the Talmudic tradition and/or codified instruments. There are also 'extraordinary places', as Esin Örücü names them, like Hong Kong or Hungary, where the Civil Law basis developed without a proper civil code and was then replaced by socialist law (and then by the recent legal developments).

Even the original Common Law was not 'pure', as it interacted with Roman law, which was already being studied at Cambridge and Oxford in the Middle Ages. It entered into contact with Talmudic law for commerce and embedded models comparable to those in Islamic law. Similarities involve different aspects: the Inns of Court (like the bar), for instance, were attached to churches, not so differently from the way in which Islamic schools were attached to mosques. Also, the way of thinking of the original juries, the 'right reason', partially overlaps conceptually with the 'analogical reasoning' of the Islamic tradition.

Interpretation plays a major role in several traditions. The divine origin of the basic sources of Talmudic and Islamic Law makes the interpretation and the updating through individuals' activity fundamental, while explaining why the law permeates the relationship of individuals with God, with others, and with authorities. In the Hindu tradition, the interpretation provided in the *Dharmashastra* is essential. The exegesis is not mediated by 'public authorities' in Talmudic, Islamic, Hindu, or African laws. Instead, the message has to reach people by word of mouth. The community's understanding of the law becomes more important than the authority's imposition in all the above-mentioned traditions.

Non-Western systems also show that personal laws are fundamental tools for preserving a tradition on an individual or a collective basis. And far from being outdated legal tools, personal laws are being debated and adopted in Europe and in the Americas as a way to accommodate migrants during an era of massive movement.

Circulation of ideas has long been (perceived as) unidirectional, because a 'ranking' of legal traditions was embraced, also mentioned in Chapter 2. The colonizers' assumed superiority, which made Western law the benchmark for what the law should be and deemed anything else as non-law, still appears in modern assessments of comparative traditions. In this respect, Menski highlights the assumption that post-colonial Africans would have no proper religious, cultural, or legal traditions to rely upon, and therefore would be obliged to pursue development and modernization exclusively along Western lines. Critical scholarship aims to overcome Western and colonial biases, embracing the viewpoint of comparatively 'marginalized' orders, also arguing that 'post-colonial' should be a descriptive and not an evaluative term.

Different streams of comparison have contributed to this trend of enhancing the geographical scope of comparative law. In addition to the assumed superiority and the reliance on established Western comparative assessments of traditions which only focused on Civil and Common Law, the 'law and development' approach has played a role in this respect as well. It defends the argument that Western law (particularly American) should be exported to catalyse legal and economic development, fostering legal transplants from the Global North into the Global South.

Finally, the Western conception of law, which prevails in comparative scholarship and is based on categories such as 'obligatory' or 'forbidden', has little or no space in the majority of traditions. Individual obligations (before God) are blurry concepts in the Talmudic and Islamic traditions and they are far from chthonic societies, whereas duty is more present in the Hindu tradition and in the Confucian idea of the *li*. Individual rights, as they are understood in the West, are also not central in the other traditions. Even the evolutionary conception of the law, over time, does not apply in the chthonic or Hindu traditions, which understand time as a circular phenomenon.

In Africa, as in chthonic law in general, dispute resolution is fundamental for understanding and arranging the existence of customary norms in modern states whose boundaries often do not reflect the actual distribution of social groups. Customary courts are established alongside Westernized state courts, which in some areas have to rely on traditions and customs. Similar to the original Common Law, authority norms are 'procedural' and the chthonic dimension determines its substance.

The Islamic legal tradition also shares the threat of other traditions, namely the imposition of Western models and the impact of colonial history (in Asia and Africa), as well as the need to find recognition within contemporary states. Hindu Law too is struggling to find its positioning regarding state law, which hardly affects the mentality and cultural heritage coming from it.

Ultimately, contemporary understandings of traditions have opened us up to the possibility of also accepting that specific national legal systems cannot be defined by simply referring to a single tradition. The concept of tradition provides normative information and allows for each concrete system to combine such information with that of other traditions. As Glenn explains, legal traditions influence each other without displacing one another.

Chapter 4
Methods and approaches

Legal comparison has a long history. Since ancient times, a comparative understanding of alternative rules has been the way for pondering the best legal institutions. In *Politics*, Aristotle compared distinctive types of constitution and discussed the merits of different forms of government in order to improve the political structure of society. In *Laws*, Plato debated the institutional framework for the imagined Cretan colony of *Magnesia* by comparing the rules of many city states to show how different organizations may result in happy and virtuous citizens (he opts for a mixed regime made up of democratic and autocratic principles). The list of legal comparativists *avant la lettre* is a long one, and it includes prominent figures from the past, from Cicero to Montesquieu.

Despite this noble history, only in the last part of the 19th century did a debate begin about the quest to provide the field of comparative law with the precise model and the settled direction it requires if it is to develop, as declared during the Paris Congress. Making legal comparison a discipline involves an understanding of alternative modes, purposes, content, and standards of evaluation for comparative inquiry. In short, making comparative law a discipline requires an accredited methodology.

At the Paris Congress, a dispute arose between those who considered comparative law a discipline and those who saw it as a method, which entailed applying comparative methodology developed in other fields to the legal one, but there is little interest in this argument in recent years. The search for a single method for comparison is blamed for offering a reductionist approach that leaves unanswered the foundational questions regarding how comparative law should be carried out. Also, there has never been a shared canon for comparison, and comparative endeavours have involved the adoption of different methods. In its short history, the comparative method actually consisted of a variety of methods for looking at law which change depending on divergences in goals and purposes, techniques, and subject matters.

Away from the 'heaven of concepts'

Although a 'one-size-fits-all' methodology has never existed, comparative studies share a common, widely accepted departure point, namely, a reaction against conceptualism, positivism, and essentialism that dominated legal disciplines in the 19th and most of the 20th century. Initially addressed to the French École de l'Exégèse—a movement that professed a strict interpretation of national law and faith in the legislative text—this anti-conceptualistic stance became the fundamental methodological basis for comparative law. Not relying on what the German lawyer Rudolf von Jhering defined as the 'heaven of concepts' and purging the research of all the dogmatic peculiarities of national legal systems are the necessary starting points for any comparative endeavour. Legal comparison cannot rely on abstract concepts and apparent similarities based on terminology. Moving above national legal categories and doctrinal structures is the first step towards making a meaningful comparison and the first rule of thumb for an inquiry that is not clouded by theoretical notions and linguistic traps.

This refutation of the primacy of dogmas and concepts, and the critique of legal classicism and formalism, are not an option in comparative law. They are rooted in the same possibility for making comparison. Concepts and categories are not fit for this purpose because they possess different attributes in different laws that a nominalist comparison may fail to identify. We cannot compare the English term *contract* with the French term *contrat*, as the English term denotes something different from the French (for example, the former does not include donation). Similarly, the English term *property* encompasses corporeal and incorporeal things, while the equivalent German term *Eigentum* is only for corporeal property. In the same vein, the English term *murder* does not contain all the cases of the French term *le meurtre*, some of which may fall within *manslaughter* under English law.

As in the cases of terms like *contract*, *property*, or *murder*, a literal translation is still possible by approximation. However, this translation does not include the full equivalence of the translated concepts. In other cases, differences are so significant as to make terms untranslatable. The characteristic Common Law notion of *trust*—interests in property divided between an administrator and others—has no equivalent concept in continental Europe. The best way to convey its meaning is to leave the term in English. In all cases, whether or not a translation is desirable, a comparison merely based on concepts would miss crucial differences in the substance of laws.

The rise of functionalism

If we want to describe distinctive laws in a clear and comprehensible way for lawyers belonging to any legal system, we need to focus on something other than contingent and variable categories. Once it is realized that abstract categories are not fit for comparison, the critical challenge for the nascent discipline is to seek an invariant, universal language that could provide an unbiased and objective framework for contrasting different laws, making comparison feasible. Against this backdrop, the principal objective of the discipline becomes the identification of a *tertium comparationis*, a neutral referent that all the entities to compare have in common.

This search for *tertium comparationis* did not develop through highly theoretical disputes within academic circles. Quite the opposite, it was primarily elaborated to solve practical problems in legal practice, and to address the difficulties of handling the clash of national legal categories in international cases. The lawyer commonly accredited with having laid the foundational basis of the comparative methodology is Ernst Rabel, an Austrian scholar who emigrated to the United States during the Nazi regime. Thanks to his unique experience as a judge on the Mixed Arbitral Tribunal Panel that adjudicated controversies arising from the Versailles Peace Treaty, and as a member of the Permanent Court for International Justice, with his studies on characterization problems in conflict of laws he provided the essential methodology for post-war comparative law.

According to Rabel, to make rules and institutions of different legal systems comparable, lawyers cannot make exclusive reference to abstract concepts and blackletter rules. Instead, they must move on to their effects and to the underlying social problems that those concepts and rules address. They must analyse how legal systems tackle a definite social problem by contrasting rules and institutions that cope with the same problem in different legal systems. As Rabel puts it: 'Rather than comparing fixed data and isolated paragraphs, we compare the solutions produced by one state for a specific factual situation with those produced by another state for the same factual situation, and then we ask why they were produced and what success they had.'

Despite relevant conceptual differences in national legal systems, the function of legal concepts and rules in specific life situations is the common feature that makes comparison possible. This problem-based formulation is far more appropriate than the formalities of legal doctrine, as it avoids the bias and distortion of a comparative analysis based on concepts.

These caveats on the clash of categories in international contexts became the methodological foundation for comparative inquiries, and comparative law adopted functionalism as its basic methodology. As Zweigert and Kötz posited, since 'the only things which are comparable are those which fulfil the same function', the right research question for legal comparison is to ask which institutions and practices fulfil similar problem-solving functions in the legal systems under scrutiny. Contrasting institutions that perform the same function is what ensures comparability, and the primary task of comparison is to find out how different legal systems solve the same socio-legal problem.

Societal needs and problems may play the role of a constant element, of a neutral referent for comparison, since they are deemed universal. The reference to the function and the belief in the universality of problems make comparison feasible. If we assume that problems are universal, it hardly happens that the foreign system has no response to a problem. Far more probably, a situation designated by a concept or an area of law in one legal system may be captured by different categories in another. This is why functionalists warn the novice not to jump to the conclusion that a foreign system has 'nothing to report' on a given issue. This conclusion is quite possibly inaccurate, since a beginner may be looking for the rule in which she is interested in the wrong place, i.e., in the area where she expects it to be under her legal system.

For example, medical malpractice is classified under contract or tort law in different legal systems. Defamation can be a private or a criminal offence. The protection of a surviving spouse may be regulated by the law of succession or by family law. Further, a single institution may tackle a problem in a legal system that a plurality of institutions tackles in other legal systems. In Civil Law, several institutions—relating to property law, family law, succession law, charities, company law, and unjust enrichment—address the issues that *trust* deals with in Common Law. Similarly, the Muslim *mahr*, an institution analogous to a dowry the husband pays to the bride, can be traced back to very different areas of law in the Western legal tradition: marital property, divorce, or contract law. Even more so, the same problem may be tackled in legal terms in one system and by customs, social or religious norms in another (for example, social stigma may be as effective as legal norms in coping with hate speech). In all these cases, different legal systems face the same problem by taking different paths. Still, these paths are functionally comparable if the focus is on problems instead of concepts.

Along this line, in the late 1950s, the German-American scholar Rudolf Schlesinger refined this method with the so-called case (or factual) approach. As a professor at Cornell, he launched a massive, ten-year project that involved lawyers from all over the world to explain how a given pattern of facts would be assessed in their legal systems. The highly technical topic chosen for this comparative inquiry was the formation of a contract. To ensure that national rapporteurs gave comparable answers, Schlesinger formulated questions in factual terms, as exemplified by case studies. According to Schlesinger, posing issues in functional terms entails freeing the analysis from abstract terms and 'conceptual cubicles' in which each legal system stores its law, and focusing on the 'concrete problem' to be tackled and on real life situations. Known as the Cornell Project, the factual approach became a reference point in post-war comparative law, and it is still followed in significant collective comparative research, such as the Common Core of European Private Law project.

A search for the structure of law

In detecting which institutions and practices are functionally equivalent, the comparativists must track whatever moulds or affects the living law, and investigate the entire context and all the factors that might influence the rules that address the problem under investigation. This reference to the many factors that constitute the legal system has been elaborated and made popular by Rodolfo Sacco. His 'dynamic approach' supplemented functionalism with a structural comparison grounded on a comprehensive understanding of what constitutes a source of law.

The formative factors of a legal system—that Sacco termed 'legal formants', a word borrowed from phonetics—denote the many elements at work in any system, giving form to the law by structuring it, from economic factors to patterns of reasoning. In detecting the formants of a legal system, Sacco challenges the official theory of legal sources. According to his functional-structural theory, comparativists cannot rely exclusively on what the lawyers of the target system would treat as a recognized, official source of law. All the formative elements of a legal system are relevant, no matter whether they are officially recognized as a legal source or not: statutory law and case law, but also academic writings, standard form contracts, general conditions of business, unwritten trade usage and customs, among others.

Even more importantly, his structural analysis questions the consistency of national legal systems. Positivism portrayed national laws as composed of a pyramid of norms hierarchically ordered, and the interpreter's task as applying these rules consistently by solving a conflict between (apparently) contradictory rules by interpretation. By contrast, the dynamic approach establishes that there is no such thing as a unity of national law made up of a coherent system of sources of law, with a single answer provided to a legal problem. As Sacco concludes, there is no guarantee that multiple legal formants will be in harmony rather than competition.

A dynamic approach to comparative law

If legal formants are often conflicting, it makes little sense to search for *the* legal rule that a legal system provides on a specific issue. All formants must be examined to ascertain how a system deals with that issue, because each formant may provide a different response to the same question.

Sacco illustrates his thesis by giving an example about workers' unions under Italian law. The Italian constitution states that workers' unions can enter into an agreement that is binding for all workers only once they are officially registered. However, statutory law has never provided a way for unions to register. In turn, courts regularly enforce agreements that unregistered unions have entered into, making these contracts binding for all workers. A positivistic account postulates the consistency of these different formants and explains apparent divergences by way of interpretation. But a more sceptical attitude reveals that constitutional rule, statutory rule, and judicial rule give conflicting answers to the same question.

By putting the accent on practical solutions, on the implementation of legal rules and on how legal agents actually deal with real life cases, the dynamic approach emphasizes that the way blackletter rules actually work depends on what legal agents—judges, scholars, lawyers, or people in business—do with these rules. This is why, especially in those legal systems that only recognize statutory law as a source of law, this approach is credited with having complemented the traditional study of blackletter rules with a focus on how rules are interpreted and applied in practice.

At the same time, the structuralist analysis gives the same foundational role to the formal expression of legal rules and to their actual implementation: to the law as described and the law as applied. According to Sacco, the legal discourse is made up of 'operative formants', whose function is to provide the working rule, but it is also made up of 'theoretical formants', whose main function is to justify and rationalize the operational rules or to convey the ideology behind them. A rule that states that parents represent their minor children is a theoretical formant that explains the operative rule that confers on parents the power to manage the property of their minor children. Both these rules are relevant in assessing how a legal system deals with the property of minor children.

The lack of harmony among formants also applies to the practical and the theoretical formants. Theoretical formants do not always say the same things as operative formants, and what legal agents do may be different from what they say they do. 'The way rules are stated may be different from the way they are enforced.' Accordingly, there is a need to track both descriptive formants and operational rules. This need is patent in comparative analysis. How is it possible to explain that rules formulated in the same way in different countries produce dissimilar practical applications? If different blackletter rules lead to the same outcome in two countries, is the law of the two countries the same?

An example on medical malpractice is frequently used to clarify this point. Medical malpractice is treated as a breach of contract under French law. This means that a strict rule of liability applies, and the victim does not need to prove fault to get compensated. The opposite holds in the United States, where medical malpractice is a tort. Accordingly, the victim must allege the fault of the tortfeasor as a ground for liability. If we limit our analysis to the formal expression of legal rules (so-called theoretical formants), the two systems give opposite solutions to the same problem. But the conclusion changes if we consider practical, working rules. Without formally contradicting the general rule, French courts established that, in non-routine cases, a doctor is under a simple duty to use her professional skills as best she can (*obligation de moyen*). If she has done this, she is not liable for not having granted the result (*obligation de résultat*). This means that the victim must prove the doctor's fault, i.e., the lack of professional skills, to demonstrate the breach. In turn, American courts fine-tuned the general rule based on negligence in routine cases by adopting the *res ipsa loquitur* ('the thing speaks for itself') doctrine, which assumes the fault of the doctor when damage occurs. Under this doctrine, negligence is implicit when not achieving a desired result. Hence, on both sides of the Atlantic, a strict rule of liability applies to routine cases, and a fault-based liability applies to non-routine cases. If we restrict the comparative analysis to the formal expression of legal rules, France and the US seem to follow opposite paths. Yet, the two systems converge on a practical level.

Where different rules produce the same practical result, or where the opposite occurs with the same rules producing divergent practical results, Sacco believes that there is often an unformulated, implicit formant. A structural analysis may underscore these tacit and non-explicit formative elements that constitute the silent, invisible dimensions of law. Though less visible, these 'implicit patterns'—which Sacco refers to as a 'cryptotype', a term borrowed from the American linguist Benjamin Lee Whorf—often shape the law even more forcefully than visible ones. Local lawyers are often not aware of and not able to formulate these tacit rules. But comparison helps them emerge, since a rule implicit in one system may play an open role in another.

Cultural immersion

Despite its fight against formalism, conceptualism, and positivism, in the last half of the 20th century, functional comparison started to be accused of being positivistic in substance and simplistic in method. Functionalism has been attacked for including a professed faith in objectivity and a deceptive quest for neutral comparison. The belief in an unbiased perspective, made possible by posing the same question to different laws, gives the illusion of an external framework that ensures a perfect comparison. The functionalist account of law as a kind of technical knowledge employed to solve social problems is blamed for not taking the many dimensions of law into appropriate consideration. Its search for neutrality and objectivity from an external observer's viewpoint is seen as grounded in an outdated version of the law as a science that ignores the complexity of the law.

In the last decade of the 20th century, a new wave of critical and cultural comparative law scholars came to the fore, reproaching functionalists for overlooking the point that understanding is moulded by categories and that categories are contingent and related to cultural contexts. Accordingly, the claim to have found an objective and universal comparison that is free from preconception, critical evaluation, and value judgement is flawed. Like every human being, comparativists have biases, interests, and prejudices. Far from being neutral and objective, comparative inquiries face significant hermeneutical hurdles, and those who pretend to offer a neutral gaze on other laws are stuck within their (mostly Western) conceptual framework and culture.

The same possibility of isolating facts as objective elements, assumed to be common to different jurisdictions, is misguided. This 'functionalist fallacy', as Günter Frankenberg termed it, is grounded on the illusory assumption that factual situations are common elements and neutral referents that cut across jurisdictions and societies. But this search for 'brute facts' is pointless since factual situations are socially constructed, and therefore different in different places. The 'same' fact is not the same if procedure and evidence differ. Even more significantly, facts are influenced by the history, mores, and ethos of different communities.

From these criticisms, comparative law began to place emphasis on an understanding of law as a cultural phenomenon, on pre-comprehension and on hermeneutics, and to focus on the historical and philosophical dimensions of law, and on a more interdisciplinary approach. Like literature, art, or music, law is a social construct embedded in culture and rooted in history, and understanding a legal system is closely akin to understanding a culture. This is why comparative law should make a cultural analysis of mentalities and the deep structures of law, with its often unexpressed ideologies, narratives, and justifications. Only by adopting this kind of 'cultural criticism' can comparative legal thinking unleash its subversive potential, as George Fletcher advocates, and comparative law can make its contribution to challenging the most established assumptions in law.

Comparativists cannot pretend to be pure, neutral spectators because no common measure for objective comparison exists in cross-cultural analysis. In opposition to the external glance posited by functionalism, the new scholarship aims to understand foreign law on its own terms. This insider view aspires to appreciate the targeted culture in an untranslated form, i.e., as the participants of that system do, in order to get a sense of their thoughts and beliefs. As cultural anthropologists, comparativists must recognize subjectivity and cultural ties and decentre their personal point of view, breaking loose from the influence of their native culture. This process of emancipation from personal beliefs, biases, and settled knowledge is a necessary step in practising what Vivian Curran terms a 'cultural immersion' in the political, historical, economic, and linguistic context that shapes the law under investigation.

In this regard, the process of decodifying foreign law is close to that of a translation. In literary works, words cannot be translated without alteration unless an entire language and culture are transported around them. The same holds for legal comparison.

As in translation, distortion is inevitable. The act of comparison is doomed to lose and betray the original meaning, transmitting only part of it (*traduire, c'est trahir*). Not only might comparativists translate legal concepts and technical words only by approximation, since these concepts are not entirely equivalent, as functionalism already posited. More radically, legal concepts are culturally bound, and any attempt to translate them inevitably loses the genius of the original language and the particular world perspective of the target culture.

This impossibility of gaining a perfect understanding and the inability to reach definitive, conclusive answers do not make legal comparison impossible. What comparativists can do is to engage in a legal translation aimed at attaining the best possible overlap with the minimum loss of significance. They must try to be the voice of the target system, 'albeit with a non-native accent', as John Bell suggests. Although imperfect, this internal perspective is far better than the imaginary neutral approach posited by functionalism, as it avoids projecting assumptions and pre-understanding onto the objects under investigation.

What is it like to try a rat?

In 1522 an ecclesiastical court in Bourgogne placed a mischief of rats on trial and charged them with a felony for having eaten and destroyed some barley crops. The bishop's vicar of the city formally summoned the rats and appointed Barthelemy Chassenée, one of the most renowned jurists of the time, to defend them. When the rats failed to appear in court, Chassenée made refined procedural arguments to justify his clients. A single writ—he sustained—was patently inadequate to give due notice to his many clients, dispersed in the entire region. A second and a third summons were needed in light of the time required to prepare their great migration and the perils of the journey for such unpopular clients. Before these irrefutable difficulties, the court adjourned the question *sine die* and judgement was finally granted for the rats.

These processes were far from extraordinary in Europe. Hundreds of cases are reported from the 9th to the 19th century, with beetles, caterpillars, pigeons, and all sorts of animals placed on trial (Figure 5). The same Chassenée published a successful treatise on the criminal prosecution of animals, full of erudite references spanning from Aristotle to Moses. The book addressed central questions regarding animal trials, such as whether they are to be considered clergy or laity (he concludes for a rebuttable presumption for laity). The success of the book, proved by its reprintings, suggests that it was more than a *divertissement*, it was tackling an actual legal need of the time.

What was it like to try a rat? William Ewald used the case of animal trials to illustrate what a comparative analysis should entail. Thanks to historical documents, formal rules governing animal trials are clear enough. But an examination of the technical knowledge of substantive and procedural rules gives us

TRIAL OF A SOW AND PIGS AT LAVEGNY.

5. 'Trial of a Sow and Pigs at Lavegny', French illustration, 1849.

little help when we try to make sense of what made such a strange practice plausible. If we want to understand what it really meant to try a rat, we need to appreciate not only the text but also the subtext and investigate the fundamental principles, the moral sentiments, and the sensibilities of the age: 'an entire way of thinking and feeling about the world', based on attitudes, habits, customs, and beliefs about guilt, punishment, pain, responsibility, and evil.

Getting a sense for the animal trials is like appreciating a foreign legal system. An understanding based on blackletter rules and practices is required, but it is not enough. The philosophical principles that lie below the surface of the rules and the internal structure of legal knowledge are far more essential for reaching an inner understanding of what justifies and motivates legal practices. This need to go beyond formal rules is manifest in bizarre legal practices such as the prosecution of rats. But it is no less crucial in any comparative endeavour, even when dealing with contemporary legal rituals that may appear less radically alien to the observer.

A visit to the cannibals, but away from the cauldron

'If I were to visit the cannibals, I would try to know as much as possible about them, but I would stay away from the cauldron.' According to Pierre Legrand, this advice by the comparative religions and comparative linguistics scholar Georges Dumézil fully applies to comparative law.

Mastering the 'inner' perspective is the necessary starting point for any comparative endeavour. Comparativists must describe foreign law in local terms if they want to understand its internal logic and mentalities and to have a grasp from the inside of what it is like to be a participant in that legal system.

However, this inner perspective is not enough. In addition, comparativists must find a way to step back and distance themselves from the culture in which they have been immersed for the investigation, and regain an external view. In other words, comparativists should get rid of not only their own original cultural biases but also those deriving from the foreign culture in which they have been immersed.

The reason why the inner account is, at best, incomplete, if not misleading, is correlated to the symbolic dimension of law and with its normative beliefs and justifications. Any legal system provides a self-description, offered by local practitioners and lawyers, which is often deceptive. An investigation into how a legal community depicts itself is crucial to show how many legal myths are perpetuated, with local informants as messengers offering the most attractive account of their legal culture. An external perspective may challenge this self-description and shed light on the target culture in ways that those within it cannot perceive, unveiling those unarticulated, unconscious aspects of that culture that are so entrenched as to be hardly perceptible to its members.

James Whitman illustrated this argument by comparing dignitary law in Europe and the United States of America. The European account typically contrasts the paramount importance of 'human dignity' and 'personal honour' in Europe, as reflected in many fields of law—privacy, death penalty, hate speech, biotechnologies, or criminal punishment, among others—with the comparatively minor role played by the same values in the United States. Europeans usually explain this difference by pointing to the violations of human dignity perpetrated by Nazi and Fascist regimes and the steady reaction of European countries after the Second World War.

According to Whitman, this conventional story, reiterated countless times, is a myth based on the insiders' perspective. An external glance would offer quite a different conclusion. Tracing back European dignitary law to pre-modern social hierarchies, it would reveal the fallacy of the conventional account as being an *ex-post* recharacterization of dignitary law as 'anti-Fascist'. It would also reveal that an extension of this claim to personal honour occurred during the Nazi period, moulding a distinctive kind of egalitarianism. Far from being a superior model of protection of personal dignity, European egalitarianism would be grounded on a 'levelling up', a promise for everyone to be treated like an aristocrat. As such, it would sit in sharp contrast with American egalitarianism, made up of a 'levelling down', where people stand together on the lowest rung of the social ladder. According to Whitman, Europeans rewrote their legal history in a 'normative beautification', giving a distorted and very flattering account of their law.

Not everyone agrees with this unconventional understanding of dignitary law, but the warning for comparativists is clear. Before the risks of relying on a misleading insider account, the comparativists must defend the possibility of translating the other's experience into the language of their own culture. An insider perspective is needed, but the comparativist must later regain her position as an outsider to not get snared by these invented normative reconstructions, which are often the most unchallenged facets of a legal system. If this is true, a cultural immersion from within and a cold stance from the outside are two critical aspects of comparison.

A German advantage?

In his groundbreaking work on the style of process and the structure of authority, Mirjan Damaška correlated the organization of authority with the role of procedure. Starting from the premise that 'dominant ideas about the role of government inform views on the purpose of justice', Damaška contrasted two ideal types. The first one, epitomized by Common Law, is based on a coordinate principle of authority and a reactive state. Under this framework, conflict resolution represents a contest among private citizens, with the judge playing a limited role. The second one, exemplified by Civil Law, displays a hierarchical style of process and an activist state. Under this framework, the state exercises its power to intervene and control process, and the style of process is an inquest rather than a contest. According to Damaška, these different views on the purpose of justice 'are relevant to the choice of many procedural arguments'. For example, in Civil Law, litigators are only 'law adversaries', whereas, in Common Law, private parties are 'law-and-fact adversaries' in charge of investigating the relevant facts and gathering and producing the factual material for adjudication.

Before these relevant differences, can comparison conclude that a legal system is better than others with regard to specific issues? In principle, by taking the function that rules perform as *tertium comparationis*, functionalism makes it possible to evaluate laws and institutions in accordance with their efficacy in solving a problem. Admittedly, many functionalists are reluctant to draw normative conclusions from their analysis and believe that comparative law is a purely descriptive activity aimed at acquiring knowledge. Nonetheless, due to its reference to a specific problem or need, functionalism may bring the promise to explain which rule is superior, i.e., which rule serves a given function better.

As an example, a functional comparison of procedural rules may conclude that delegating the search for facts to judges, as in European non-adversarial procedure, may be better than the 'adversary domination' typical of the Common Law. Such a system would bear fewer incentives to distort evidence, lower expenses for the parties, and fewer complexities for the system. As a better model, it may be an inspiration for a civil justice reform in the United States that confers the main responsibility for gathering and sifting evidence to courts.

The picture changes if we see law as the outcome of a cultural tradition and collective identity. Under this perspective, dispute resolution models are the product and the reflection of national culture, and are expressive of the peculiar relationship between individuals and authority. Thus, a debate on the best model for civil procedure could not be disputed under supposedly universal rationality because law is not merely a neutral function performed by the rule. Legal reforms are culturally bound, and they must be placed in a cultural context and examined in historical and symbolic terms.

Framed this way, the supposed willingness of Germans to accept structures of authority, with its paternalistic and bureaucratic judge, would be profoundly at odds with American culture. Americans could never adopt the supposed 'German advantage' in civil procedure, as John Langbein advocated, because such a legal reform would affect crucial aspects of American legal culture. In turn, critics reply that it is doubtful whether the American and the German attitudes to litigation are so unique and distinctive, insinuating that cultural differences often become the universal apologetic for maintaining the status quo when criticism is made based on comparison.

Quantitative comparative law

In recent times, a pragmatic and quantitative version of functionalism pushed the assessment of the function of legal rules and the search for the best solution a step further. Inspired by the work of the economist Hernando de Soto, a group of law and finance scholars—commonly known as Legal Origins—started to use legal comparison to assess the degree of regulation for business and the extent to which economic agents are free to behave in the market.

Legal Origins ground their analysis on an empirical evaluation of the legal systems and their institutions, as revealed by standardized measures: the time and cost to enforce a contract, go through bankruptcy, trade across borders, or register and transfer commercial property. Thanks to these quantitative indicators, Legal Origins proclaim that they are able to compare the relative merits of national laws in terms of economic growth and economic performance, gauge regulatory outcomes, and even measure the effect of national laws on market efficiency and countries' competitiveness.

Another crucial aspect of this stream of scholarship is in reference to the country's 'legal origins' (hence the name). Legal Origins claim to be able not only to contrast but also to rank countries based on market efficiency, with those that regulate the least placed at the top of the ranking. In doing this, Legal Origins returned to the traditional classification based on legal families. In their account, the belonging of a country to one or another legal family is the most relevant reason for economic development. Against this backdrop, their studies aim at unveiling the relationship between legal families, the extent of economic regulation, and the efficiency of each legal system. According to their findings, Civil Law countries and former Socialist countries are deemed to be those who regulate the most, creating a less market-friendly environment for firms. In contrast, Common Law and Scandinavian countries are considered to be the most efficient model of legal evolution.

With its emphasis on the importance of legal rules in fostering economic development, this particular version of functionalism goes far beyond the conventional one, adopting a stringently deterministic assessment of legal regulations. Also, using standardized cases, figures, and indicators, it transforms the immaterial qualities of a legal system into objective and measurable elements.

Despite its many pitfalls, this oversimplified type of functionalism proved to be highly successful both within academia, especially in fields like comparative corporate law, and beyond it. Explicitly designed to assist law reformers in adopting the supposedly 'best' solutions and to improve countries' competitiveness, the writings of Legal Origins turned out to be very appealing to law reformers worldwide in assessing the quality of law and legal institutions, with the aim of designing institutional reforms in the name of market efficiency.

In this regard, Legal Origins inspired the Doing Business Report (Figure 6). Published every year since 2003 by the World Bank,

Rank	Economy	DB score	Rank	Economy	DB score	Rank	Economy	DB score
1	New Zealand	86.8	65	Puerto Rico (U.S.)	70.1	128	Barbados	57.9
2	Singapore	86.2	66	Brunei Darussalam	70.1	129	Ecuador	57.7
3	Hong Kong SAR, China	85.3	67	Colombia	70.1	130	St. Vincent and the Grenadines	57.1
4	Denmark	85.3	68	Oman	70.0	131	Nigeria	56.9
5	Korea, Rep.	84.0	69	Uzbekistan	69.9	132	Niger	56.8
6	United States	84.0	70	Vietnam	69.8	133	Honduras	56.3
7	Georgia	83.7	71	Jamaica	69.7	134	Guyana	55.5
8	United Kingdom	83.5	72	Luxembourg	69.6	135	Belize	55.5
9	Norway	82.6	73	Indonesia	69.6	136	Solomon Islands	55.3
10	Sweden	82.0	74	Costa Rica	69.2	137	Cabo Verde	55.0
11	Lithuania	81.6	75	Jordan	69.0	138	Mozambique	55.0
12	Malaysia	81.5	76	Peru	68.7	139	St. Kitts and Nevis	54.6
13	Mauritius	81.5	77	Qatar	68.7	140	Zimbabwe	54.5
14	Australia	81.2	78	Tunisia	68.7	141	Tanzania	54.5
15	Taiwan, China	80.9	79	Greece	68.4	142	Nicaragua	54.4
16	United Arab Emirates	80.9	80	Kyrgyz Republic	67.8	143	Lebanon	54.3
17	North Macedonia	80.7	81	Mongolia	67.8	144	Cambodia	53.8
18	Estonia	80.6	82	Albania	67.7	145	Palau	53.7
19	Latvia	80.3	83	Kuwait	67.4	146	Grenada	53.4
20	Finland	80.2	84	South Africa	67.0	147	Maldives	53.3
21	Thailand	80.1	85	Zambia	66.9	148	Mali	52.9
22	Germany	79.7	86	Panama	66.6	149	Benin	52.4
23	Canada	79.6	87	Botswana	66.2	150	Bolivia	51.7
24	Ireland	79.6	88	Malta	66.1	151	Burkina Faso	51.4
25	Kazakhstan	79.6	89	Bhutan	66.0	152	Mauritania	51.1
26	Iceland	79.0	90	Bosnia and Herzegovina	65.4	153	Marshall Islands	50.9
27	Austria	78.7	91	El Salvador	65.3	154	Lao PDR	50.8
28	Russian Federation	78.2	92	San Marino	64.2	155	Gambia, The	50.3
29	Japan	78.0	93	St. Lucia	63.7	156	Guinea	49.4
30	Spain	77.9	94	Nepal	63.2	157	Algeria	48.6
31	China	77.9	95	Philippines	62.8	158	Micronesia, Fed. Sts.	48.1
32	France	76.8	96	Guatemala	62.6	159	Ethiopia	48.0
33	Turkey	76.8	97	Togo	62.3	160	Comoros	47.9
34	Azerbaijan	76.7	98	Samoa	62.1	161	Madagascar	47.7
35	Israel	76.7	99	Sri Lanka	61.8	162	Suriname	47.5
36	Switzerland	76.6	100	Seychelles	61.7	163	Sierra Leone	47.5
37	Slovenia	76.5	101	Uruguay	61.5	164	Kiribati	46.9
38	Rwanda	76.5	102	Fiji	61.5	165	Myanmar	46.8
39	Portugal	76.5	103	Tonga	61.4	166	Burundi	46.8
40	Poland	76.4	104	Namibia	61.4	167	Cameroon	46.1
41	Czech Republic	76.3	105	Trinidad and Tobago	61.3	168	Bangladesh	45.0
42	Netherlands	76.1	106	Tajikistan	61.3	169	Gabon	45.0
43	Bahrain	76.0	107	Vanuatu	61.1	170	São Tomé and Príncipe	45.0
44	Serbia	75.7	108	Pakistan	61.0	171	Sudan	44.8
45	Slovak Republic	75.6	109	Malawi	60.9	172	Iraq	44.7
46	Belgium	75.0	110	Côte d'Ivoire	60.7	173	Afghanistan	44.1
47	Armenia	74.5	111	Dominica	60.5	174	Guinea-Bissau	43.2
48	Moldova	74.4	112	Djibouti	60.5	175	Liberia	43.2
49	Belarus	74.3	113	Antigua and Barbuda	60.3	176	Syrian Arab Republic	42.0
50	Montenegro	73.8	114	Egypt, Arab Rep.	60.1	177	Angola	41.3
51	Croatia	73.6	115	Dominican Republic	60.0	178	Equatorial Guinea	41.1
52	Hungary	73.4	116	Uganda	60.0	179	Haiti	40.7
53	Morocco	73.4	117	West Bank and Gaza	60.0	180	Congo, Rep.	39.5
54	Cyprus	73.4	118	Ghana	60.0	181	Timor-Leste	39.4
55	Romania	73.3	119	Bahamas, The	59.9	182	Chad	36.9
56	Kenya	73.2	120	Papua New Guinea	59.8	183	Congo, Dem. Rep.	36.2
57	Kosovo	73.2	121	Eswatini	59.5	184	Central African Republic	35.6
58	Italy	72.9	122	Lesotho	59.4	185	South Sudan	34.6
59	Chile	72.6	123	Senegal	59.3	186	Libya	32.7
60	Mexico	72.4	124	Brazil	59.1	187	Yemen, Rep.	31.8
61	Bulgaria	72.0	125	Paraguay	59.1	188	Venezuela, RB	30.2
62	Saudi Arabia	71.6	126	Argentina	59.0	189	Eritrea	21.6
63	India	71.0	127	Iran, Islamic Rep.	58.5	190	Somalia	20.0
64	Ukraine	70.2						

6. **Ranking of business regulation in 190 economies (Doing Business 2020 by the World Bank Group).**

this once very influential publication underscored regulatory obstacles to business, identified what might be reformed, and offered a comprehensive benchmark for assessing regulation. Strongly contested for its methodological flaws and lack of transparency, the publication of the report was finally stopped in 2021, following an independent investigation that found the drafters of the report had manipulated data and inflated rankings and scores for some countries.

A way of life or a rule of thumb?

If functionalism is censured for a lack of sophistication and for representing a reductionist approach to law which is unable to explain the complexity of law, the opposite accusation is often made to the new wave of scholarship. Postmodernists, culturalists, and critical scholars are pointed out as the main culprits for the obscurity of contemporary comparative legal scholarship and for being overly demanding.

Their call to consider law as part of the legal culture is criticized for having transformed comparative law into an elitist intellectual challenge for the sake of a happy few outstanding soloists who can deal with foreign cultures and speak several languages. The obscurity of their scholarship and their inability to offer clear directives on how to make comparison are blamed for failing to provide the discipline with a practical method that can be used by ordinary human beings, making the comparativist an earnest amateur bound to always be superficial and underinformed, someone who knows very little of many things. In response, this accusation is rejected as being beside the point. As Legrand rhetorically asks, who said that comparison should be an easy task?

The debate on the complexity of comparative scholarship is not new. In the past, scholars like Frederick Lawson and Alan Watson warned that comparative law could not be systematic.

Comparative knowledge is an extremely complex activity, far easier to make than to theoretically justify. As William Twining declared, 'serious comparative study is more like a way of life than a method'.

In light of this irreducible complexity, some comparativists believe that it may be wise not to address all the conceptual and practical hurdles of comparison but to make a practical comparison based on a helpful and flexible rule of thumb. After all, the founding fathers of the discipline were more interested pragmatically than methodologically. Rabel himself was mostly concerned with developing a viable strategy that was in line with practice-oriented objectives—choice of law and legal harmonization—rather than in making a detailed elaboration and theoretical framework of a methodology.

Admittedly, it is quite difficult to defend the orthodox version of functionalism from the accusation of positivism and lack of sophistication: a naïve faith in the possibility of grasping objective reality, its quest for a neutral framework, and the tendency to see the law in terms of causal explanations based on a sharp distinction between facts and effects. Even less defensible is the methodological imperialism that made functionalism the orthodoxy of comparison and the monopolist of methodology in comparison.

However, these many limitations and theoretical flaws only make sense if we consider functionalism as a fully developed theoretical and rigorous method. But once freed from its less tenable legacy, functionalism can still play a significant role in comparative legal enquiries. Its warnings about obstacles and pitfalls in legal comparison, and the tips and strategies on how to overcome them, may not be enough to define a rigorous methodology, but they are beneficial as a simple way of looking at legal problems, as Jaakko Husa suggests. Along this line, a new wave of scholars, from James Gordley to Michele Graziadei, vindicates the most fruitful legacies of functionalism, showing how it is not necessarily at odds with the aim for a comparison attuned to diversity. In the end, the search for functional equivalents provided great comparative works and it is still the departing point for many researchers.

A gift of freedom, the most dangerous one

Do these divergences in methodology offer a fruitful dose of discord within academic circles that may give rise to an amazing polyphony? Or is the lack of a common canon in legal comparison condemning the discipline to anarchy, where 'anything goes'? When dealing with the ubiquitous (for comparativists) warning made by the German philosopher Gustav Radbruch that disciplines that are too worried about methodology are 'weak sciences' ('sciences which have to busy themselves with their own methodology are sick sciences'), the old generation of comparative lawyers have proudly proclaimed the health of their discipline and their lack of discomfort about their search for a method.

At that time, comparative law was still living its experimental stage. No longer a young discipline today, these endless disputes on methodology are increasingly seen as major concerns in a bid for the full recognition of comparative law as a discipline, and the reason why many see the discipline as a subject without a constituency, defined by Harold Gutteridge as the Cinderella of the legal sciences, in a perennial 'search for an audience' according to Basil Markesinis.

Others see this pluralism in methodology with less perplexed eyes. Despite methodological disputes, over more than a century, comparative law has collected a fantastic amount of knowledge. But even the most optimistic must admit the difficulties in combining these remarkable but eclectic pieces of knowledge into a fully coherent field due to the absence of a common denominator other than analysing more legal systems or investigating legal issues that involve foreign law. Without a shared methodology, comparative law runs the risk of remaining an ill-defined subject, a loose label applicable to any investigation that deals in some way with foreign law.

In sum, this wide range of methodological approaches for comparative endeavours is concurrently appealing and perilous, as Kahn-Freund concludes in a seminal work. The methodological richness of comparative law, he believes, must be praised as an extraordinary 'gift of freedom' for researchers. However—he also adds, citing Erich Fromm's *Escape from Freedom*—comparativists bear the full responsibility that this freedom entails.

Chapter 5
Sameness and difference

Of apples and oranges

Comparison entails an investigation of both similarities and differences. In principle, any one thing can be compared with any other thing. However, things under investigation must be similar in some respects and different in others for that comparison to be meaningful. There is not much point in comparing identical things, but it is impossible to compare things with nothing at all in common. An area of homogeneity is needed to find cases that are comparable along with specific properties. Otherwise, a lack of common measures between the two would make any comparison impossible.

The conventional apple and orange objection suggests that the similar must be compared with the similar. Yet, the soundness of the famous adage depends on how the comparison between an apple and an orange is made. The existence of an area of similarity is connected to the property considered in comparing two things. A comparison of apples and oranges may lead to different results in terms of similarity and difference, depending on the approach chosen for the comparative inquiries. For example, it is possible to compare apples and oranges according to their nutritional properties, market price, or size.

Integrative and contrastive comparison

As with the case of apples and oranges, a comparison may uncover similarities hidden behind superficial differences, and it may reveal the divergences that seemingly similar things conceal. This is why comparative law has been described as an investigation of 'the range and complexity of the differences that can lie behind a facade of similarity', or as the task of overcoming obstacles of terminology and classification 'in order to show that foreign law is not very different from ours but only appears to be so', to use the words of two prominent scholars, Arthur von Mehren and Basil Markesinis.

Against this backdrop, the debate in comparative law has been revolving around the major *principium comparationis*. Is comparative law primarily aimed at uncovering similarities and universal features across different laws, or instead at recognizing the differences among them?

Someone may ask why such a choice is needed. After all, why couldn't comparative law just remain unbiased in this regard? As Montesquieu wonders in a chapter of his *De l'esprit des lois*, 'does not a greatness of genius consist rather in distinguishing between those cases in which uniformity is requisite, and those in which there is a necessity for differences?'

However, as the case of oranges and apples teaches us, the comparativist does not uncover pre-existing differences and similarities. By choosing what matters—the objects to investigate, the variables to consider, and the purposes and focus of the analysis—she actively contributes to their construction.

Sameness and differences in legal taxonomy

The traditional classification into legal families helps to elucidate how the choices and purposes of comparative research contribute to the assessment of differences and similarities. Conventional taxonomies, as we have seen, divide all the laws of the world into families. Both inside and outside each family, this mode of classification is grounded on a binary understanding of similarities and differences. Within each legal family, supposedly homogeneous legal systems are grouped in accordance with their common features. An emphasis is put on commonalities among members, while divergences are seen as negligible departures from the same model. At the same time, different legal families are identified and categorized in accordance with characteristic features that make them utterly different from the others. Due to this intrinsic dichotomic nature, orthodox classifications oversimplify both differences and similarities. They are prone to ignoring differences within the same family and similarities among systems belonging to different families. England and India are deemed similar as both belong to the Common Law family, while Germany and England are inherently different since they belong to different legal families.

This assessment of similarities and differences among legal families and their members has changed from time to time. A stark opposition between Civil Law and Common Law was commonplace during most of the 19th and the 20th centuries. At the Paris Congress, the great majority of participants believed these two families to be so distant as to make them incomparable. The peculiar insularity of English Common Law, and its irreducible distance from the continent, was asserted by reference to both philosophical ideas and legal technicalities. Rationalism and deductive reasoning dominated continental Europe, whereas empiricism and inductive reasoning were the major forces within English culture. This picture was further reinforced by pointing to the role of English courts and their particular remedial approach, in comparison to the role of legislation and codification in continental Europe and its right-based approach. In more recent times, an opposite account has prevailed. Civil Law and Common Law have started to be deemed sub-members of a common

Western legal tradition. Rather than seeing the technical differences in their legal systems and philosophical heritage, the emphasis is placed on their analogous economic and political structures, connected to democracy and free market, and on their distinctive, historically contingent way of shaping the relationships between law, politics, religion, and morality: the rule of law, the supremacy of law over politics and religions, an understanding of law as a coherent and integrated system, a distinctive legal profession in charge of legal institutions, and a professionalized legal education.

Along the same lines, an intense debate took place during the Cold War on how distinctive Soviet law was from the 'bourgeois laws' of capitalist countries. At that time, David and most Western comparativists believed that a comparison between the two was possible, as 'the problems in the USSR and the West are often nonetheless the same, because each, in its own way, is concerned with moral, social and economic development'. In contrast, Socialist scholars disagreed that their law could be meaningfully compared with the bourgeois ones. Fundamental dissimilarities in the aims of law made the Soviet family radically different from capitalist countries and comparison impossible. In their eyes, bourgeois law was nothing more than the will of the ruling class to establish norms for governing a corrupt economic system in accordance with their desires. In sharp opposition, they described Socialist law as a means of liberating workers from exploitation and transforming society towards communist ideals. The apparent resemblance of Socialist laws to continental legal systems—they concluded—remained on the surface of law, entirely related to the terminology employed and the formal structure of law due to the Roman roots of Soviet law. But beyond this facade, the two families were irreducibly different.

As in the Civil Law versus Common Law divide, the degree of divergence or convergence between Soviet law and Western law depended on the standards chosen for comparison. The focus on purely legal criteria, such as sources of law or formal legal categories, led to a similarity between Socialist laws and Civil Law, with Soviet law as a historical deviation from the law of continental Europe. The opposite held true if the focus was put on social and economic factors.

Also, the traditional call to compare like with like contributed to the marginalization of 'non-Western' legal systems in legal taxonomies. The proclaimed impossibility of comparing strikingly dissimilar systems suggested avoiding a comparison between the law of 'civilized nations' and that of 'underdeveloped' societies and focusing instead on legal systems at the same stage of legal, political, and economic development. In turn, this marginalization led to an exoticization of Asian and African law in legal mapping, as in the conventional account of a 'traditional' Muslim law, with a common identity shared by all 'Muslims' based on their religious and legal beliefs, today as in the past. This is held to have produced what Lama Abu-Odeh defined as a 'fantasy effect' in comparative legal studies that misrepresents Islamic law and downplays differences and changes, leaving scholars from these areas of the world faced with a drastic choice between exoticism or assimilation.

Sameness and differences in comparative methodology

The dispute over methodology offers another powerful illustration of the sameness versus diversity debate in comparative legal scholarship. By postulating a parallelism of social problems across the world, functionalism displays a solid tendency to unveil similarities rather than differences. Recall that the underlying premise of functionalism is that legal rules and institutions cope with problems shared everywhere in the world. Functionalism does acknowledge the existence of formal divergences and differences, but only to find a more profound, substantial equivalence in the function. Legal systems may find quite different ways to tackle these common issues, and legal techniques may vary, but the problems of justice they face are basically the same in time and space throughout the world.

Even more radically, the strong preference for commonalities displayed by functionalism is not confined to the underlying assumption that all societies face the same problems. In its most successful version, popularized by Zweigert and Kötz, functionalism postulates that similarities among legal systems also concern the solutions that these systems reach. Not only do different societies face *similar problems*; most of the time, they also reach *similar results*. Seemingly different discourses often lead to convergent practical results because different laws give formally diverse but substantially similar responses to the same universal problems. Notably, this uniformity is often hidden, either for ideological and symbolic reasons or due to the particularity of conceptual structures and the distinctive way law is technically formulated in each legal system. But behind this apparent diversity, a functionalist analysis helps to unveil how legal systems actually work, disclosing their fundamental closeness.

In this regard, Zweigert and Kötz famously formulated their *praesumptio similitudinis*: a presumption that the practical effects of different laws are similar. In their words: 'One can almost speak of *a basic rule of comparative law*: different legal systems give the same or very similar solutions, even as to detail, to the same problem of life, despite the great differences in their historical development, conceptual structure, and style of operation.'

According to Zweigert and Kötz, the similarity is not just the most likely result of comparative enquiries, and the sameness of practical results is not just a helpful working rule. More radically, it is a means to check the outcomes of one's investigation, a heuristic principle that affirms a presumption not just of problems addressed by different societies but also of solutions reached:

the comparatist must rest content if his researches through all the relevant material lead to the conclusion that the systems he has compared reach the same or similar practical results, but if he finds that there are great differences or indeed diametrically opposite results, he should be warned and go back to check again whether the terms in which he posed his original question were indeed purely functional, and whether he has spread the net of his research quite wide enough.

Sameness and differences in legal transplants

In the same vein, the debate on legal change and the transferability of laws from one legal system to another has been deeply affected by the integrative or contrastive attitudes towards comparison. At first, the macro view adopted by historians such as Watson was dominant in the field. This understanding of the circulation of law focused on the big picture and similarities, the bulk of transplants in human history, and their social ease. Later, a more sociological approach prevailed, made of micro stories, which focused on the local context and the difficulties of such a reception of foreign law due to fundamental differences.

It is not only the scale and detail of the analysis that makes a difference. Also, in a world made of nation-states, comparison is a way to see similarities and universal traits that transcend national borders. But in a seemingly globalized world, like the one we live in today, comparison becomes an indispensable aid for uncovering profound and irreducible differences and those vital reactions that give birth to creative cultural forms in opposition to seemingly homologizing and standardizing trends.

The existence of an often-latent common core across legal systems, and the consequent search for these hidden commonalities, are challenged. The convergence of European legal systems under EU law, or the apparently inexorable globalizing trends in law, which are often taken for granted in many comparative analyses, are seen as no more than an illusion. The most visible elements may effectively converge, but such a conclusion remains at the surface of law. Beyond it, unbridgeable differences remain, making the widespread belief in a unifying trend in law a chimaera.

This emphasis on difference also questions the soundness of the many law reform programmes adopted by Western institutions and international organizations to promote economic growth, democracy, and fundamental rights. Projects of legal unification or harmonization, which were pivotal for the post-war generation of comparativists, are now criticized for putting together context-less normative propositions and legal texts, usually derived from Common Law or Civil Law, and for imposing Western values on others. As Geoffrey Samuels suggests, these projects now call to mind a kind of *capriccio* art: a legal pastiche in which culturally distant ideas are juxtaposed on the same canvas, as in William Marlow's painting Capriccio of St Paul's Cathedral on the Grand Canal (1797).

Jus unum

The original tendency of comparative legal scholarship to emphasize similarities and seek harmonization and unification of laws dominated the discipline in the 19th century and in the first part of the 20th century. The Société de Législation Comparée, founded in 1869, adopted 'Jus unum' ('One law') as its motto. In the same vein, the many scholars who gathered at the Paris Congress in 1900 unanimously concluded that comparative legal studies should be primarily aimed at discovering uniformities among various national laws, and at erecting a common law out of local particularities. Their words show a strong commitment to universality and transcendent values. 'Discipline's goal should be to retrieve from the mass of particular legal institutions a common fund, that is the points of rapprochement that may be discovered from apparently diverse elements. These points constitute the essential identity of universal legal life.' A similar 'hope of contributing to greater harmony in the principles and forms of procedure upon which *the law of civilised nations* should be based' guided the first American Congress, held in St Louis in 1904.

At that time, few doubted that the task of the discipline was uncovering the unity behind apparent divergences and to reduce the diversity of legal orders to a single set of natural-law principles. The disagreement was limited to defining the boundaries of this common core of shared principles, whether confined to the *droit commun législatif* of those nations with a comparable level of civilization, or open to a more universalist *droit commun de l'humanité*.

This tendency for comparative law to seek universals and deny differences was further reinforced after the Second World War. As Vivian Curran and David Kennedy narrate in their compelling reconstruction of the post-war generation of comparativists, the priority for sameness was not a purely academic attitude. Their personal life was crucial in this regard. Their particular background may suggest why they considered comparative research as a way to identify similarities across cultures and universal principles.

Especially in the United States, comparative law was a refugee field made by European scholars. After Hitler took power, the Nazi regime forbade these 'non-Aryan' scholars to teach at their universities, forcing them to leave Europe and flee to the United States to escape the Holocaust: Rudolf Schlesinger (Cornell), Friedrich Kessler (Yale), Ernst Rabel (Michigan), Max Rheinstein (Chicago), among others. A 'University of Exile' was established at the New School in New York where many European scholars found their home.

The roots of the academic posture of this unique generation of scholars can be traced back to these tragic events. Their personal trauma may vindicate the choice they made in their scholarship and the emphasis they put, sometimes with an overly romantic tone, on unified humanity. Nazism brought exclusion and discrimination on those who were deemed 'different', and made this 'other' the enemy. The assumption of likeness, the search for the transcendent values of law and for the universality of legal science, and the willingness to identify unifying elements and to overlook differences, were all aimed at privileging an agenda of sameness as providing the only way to tolerance, in a world where inclusion was possible only based on the likeness of people, not on the recognition of diversity.

These scholars firmly believed that comparative law could play a crucial role in their mission. In their eyes, it could support international institutions, foster mutual understanding of people, and help build a peaceful future and pursue the unity of humankind. Comparative law could help save the world from destruction.

The loss of innocence and the rise of contrastive comparison

Beyond the reasons that made the search for commonalities the main priority of comparative law, comparativists have been 'weirdly innocent of the fact that human societies differ', as James Whitman denounces. For too long they have been acting like naïve travellers, incapable of decentring their personal point of view and levelling others as a measure of themselves, with foreign law being seen as like or unlike their own. As such, they did the opposite of what a meaningful comparison should do.

In the latter part of the 20th century, it looked like the time had come for comparativists to become a different kind of traveller who is ready, not to see foreign law by the measure of their own law, but to meet the unexpected and the unknown. In response to an approach to comparative law that confined the discipline's mission to the uncovering of sameness and commonalities across legal systems, a new wave of scholars arose, more attuned to dissimilarities and divergences. Marc Ancel famously coined the notion of *comparaison contrastée* to mark this change and emphasize the primacy and persistence of differences in comparison.

In line with the cultural and hermeneutical turn in comparative legal studies, comparativists started to draw attention to the need to appreciate the depth of difference. Recognizing the significance of categories in the process of understanding, and their being contingent upon cultures, means being aware of the impact of the self and developing a sense for diversity and heterogeneity.

A 'presumption of dissimilarity' corrects the past overemphasis on similarity and replaces the *a priori* bias in favour of sameness. Making alterity the governing principle of comparison changes the way comparative law deals with taxonomy, patterns of change, and methodology. It underscores the importance of comparing radically different legal systems rather than similar ones. It challenges the ease and even the possibility of legal transplants. It puts functionalism at fault for its faith in deeper universal values that all societies share and its tendency towards uniformization that makes this method prone to an *a priori* search for universal law clouded by superficial differences. In particular, it ridicules the *praesumptio similitudinis* for assuming, rather than checking, its findings: by warning researchers to go back in cases of differences in their results, functionalism suggested a search for commonalities *ad infinitum* that supported one hypothesis over the other, making similarity the confirmation of the validity of the research.

Notably, this change of attitude in comparative legal scholarship has not been a revolt against the founding fathers of the discipline, but against their less sophisticated epigones. Those masters of comparative law were cosmopolitan and polyglot scholars. Despite their professed credo, their investigations were far from reductionist. As Vivian Curran shows, they were perfectly able to appreciate differences and practise a *de facto* cultural immersion *avant la lettre*, without the need to theorize it. Like Molière's *bourgeois gentilhomme*, who didn't know he spoke prose and was sure to speak French, they practised a sophisticated comparison *sub silentio*, attuned to differences as well as similarities. However, their legacy turned out to also be misleading for the next generations of less experienced scholars, who devotedly replicated the most superficial parts of their scholarship and methods, without having the same background, with the result of transforming that extraordinary experience into an oversimplified approach to comparison.

The Emperor Justinian before the Austrian code

'What, then, is to be compared? It comes down to what we mean by the term Law.' As Roscoe Pound recognizes, a thick versus thin understanding of law lies behind the dispute on sameness versus difference in comparative law. Differences in law can be textual or structural, but most of the time they are more deeply rooted than that. The more one thinks of law in terms of rules and functions, the more likely one is to find similarities. The more one focuses on the history, culture, and social context, the more likely one is to find epistemological and cultural differences.

The differences in what comparativists mean about the term law, and the consequences of their answers to the finding of similarities and differences, are well-illustrated by the case made by Alan Watson in a passage where he tries to clarify his theory of legal transplants. Watson wonders what the reaction of a law student in the age of the ancient Roman Emperor Justinian, trained on his *Corpus Iuris Civilis*, would be to the 19th-century Austrian civil code. In his view, the Roman student would not be so surprised by the Austrian code and concludes that differences in legal rules between ancient Rome and modern Vienna could not be termed major developments. The biggest surprise for this ancient law student would be the disappearance of a law of slavery.

What exactly is made similar in Watson's account? His conclusion of similarity of laws across centuries focuses on rules, neglecting philosophical ideals, culture, and history. With these limitations, Watson may claim that the rules of the Austrian civil code are almost identical to those of the Roman Digest and the student in the age of Justinian would not be astonished by the substance of the law. However, as Ewald suggests, such a conclusion would disregard all those aspects that would make the student from ancient Rome a perfect stranger to the contemporary world, no matter how much he might know about blackletter rules. Restricting the analysis to the formal aspects of law—blackletter rules and practical results—runs the risk of seeing similarities even where big differences exist. According to Watson, if a tomato grower sells his plants and the buyer puts them in her garden, they are still the same tomato plants despite being in different soil and sunlight. According to Legrand, it is the garden, not the individual plant, that really matters. In sum, emphasis on similarity or differences in law is, above all, the by-product of a different understanding of law.

Decolonizing comparative law

An account of similarities and differences in law is not merely an academic description, carried out in a purely technical framework. Inspired by those critical theories of law that investigate the links between law and politics, and the relationships between sameness and difference, inclusion and exclusion, in the last part of the 20th century the political agnosticism of mainstream comparative law started to be placed under scrutiny.

Although comparative law has always distanced itself from politics and ideologies, offering what Horatia Muir-Watt defines as an 'anaemic' view of law, where its political dimension is downplayed, comparative inquiries are not apolitical products of technical information. Quite the opposite, they have important political consequences and are an integral part of the fabric of global governance. For example, framing a topic as a technical issue may contribute to seeing a top-down law reform based on foreign models as a legitimate intervention. In contrast, invoking cultural diversity and irreducible distances may help to depict the same reform as an imperialistic intrusion.

Even when apparently descriptive, as in legal taxonomies, comparative law has critical political consequences, since they are crucial for how identities are constructed. As an example, Teemu Ruskola showed the colonialist attitude to comparative law by demonstrating the asymmetric relationship posited by mainstream scholarship between the United States of America and China, with the former seen as the embodiment of universal values and the latter as an expression of a particular culture. Likewise, Jorge Esquirol argued that the supposedly European character of Latin American law, advanced by conventional taxonomies, bears significant political implications. The account of Latin American legal tradition as forming part of the European legacy is typically based on a deep discordance between law and society, made up of a still illiberal society at odds with a liberal elite of jurists. Such an explanation makes 'Europeaness' a political aspiration shared by local lawyers, that helps to mobilize the legal culture to align with liberal and democratic values and to support the traditional programme of liberal democracy in Latin America, in a process of assimilation of local societies to (an often idealized) Europe.

In the same way, a postcolonial critique of the discipline denounces a field still dominated by the Global North. Rejecting the narrative of comparative law as being a young discipline—with no significant past before the 1900 Paris Congress—this postcolonial epistemology traces the intellectual roots of comparative law to the 19th century to uncover the links between imperialism, colonialism, and the production of knowledge in comparative law. It also reveals the discipline's intrinsically and often implicitly judgemental attitude.

Decolonizing comparative law means rejecting the Western worldview and the universalizing role of Western law. By using Western laws as a benchmark, with other laws categorized as similar or different, this persistently colonialist approach to mainstream comparative law relegates the non-European to a secondary racial, cultural, and ontological status. It establishes rankings and implicit hierarchies, and divides up the world in accordance with universalized Western standards. This judgemental stance explains why comparative law is depicted as emancipatory in the Global North while it is often linked to colonial oppression in the Global South.

Consequently, it is critical to scrutinize the political choices behind the technical assumptions of comparative law. The different attitudes towards centralization, decentralization, and the degree of respect for cultural differences can unveil the hidden political dimension of comparative law. In this regard, it is crucial to translate the 'shadow vocabulary'—as David Kennedy terms it—routinely employed within academic circles, to describe seemingly neutral choices and technical methodological options in political and ideological terms to be embraced or contested.

Chapter 6
What for? The uses of comparative law

A process of mutual learning

Learning from different systems has always been a relevant tool to understand, contextualize, and develop the law. Therefore, the practical dimension of comparative law has been at the core of the discipline since its start through imitations and projects of unification and harmonization at the international level. Recent phenomena, such as globalization and the spread of regional integration (the European Union, the Council of Europe, the Inter-American System of Protection of Human Rights, among others), have reinforced this dimension from a domestic perspective too, involving different actors, from legislators to judges, up to scholars. Resolving common problems in terms of ethical, economic, and social scope or timing are also fundamental driving factors into the direction of shared legal solutions, particularly when an issue is not bound by national borders. In this respect, the need to provide legal responses to digitalization and interaction via the internet, bioethical dilemmas, financial crises, pandemics, or social changes such as the emergence of new family units offers only a few examples.

Comparative law, far from being an 'intellectual luxury' that only privileged lawyers and scholars could pursue in the past, is increasingly both an intellectual and a practical tool for legislators, judges, and lawyers beyond those international commercial disputes that even the most sceptical scholars like George P. Fletcher considered as having a comparative value. This applies also to jurisdictions and university systems that have long considered themselves to be self-sufficient. Legal comparison is a meaningful addition in improving the quality of legal education while providing critical tools to better assess, understand, and amend one's own law; it is used to infuse content into legal sources through the imitation of different systems, both at constitutional and legislative levels. Judges, as well, may include in their arguments references to foreign law to reinforce their reasoning.

Private law has traditionally been more often compared, as phenomena such as international families or trade and commercial arrangements between companies from distinct countries are extremely common. Public/constitutional law, on the other hand, used to seem more resistant to foreign influence, as already underlined by Otto Kahn-Freund, but this differentiation is being diluted due to several factors favouring the circulation of ideas and imitations.

First, the abovementioned emergence of common problems has led to imitations in all fields. Additionally, the waves of constitutionalism after the Second World War were aided by the possibility of drawing inspiration from previous generations of constitutions, picking foreign solutions and possibly mixing them. The approval of numerous international treaties regulating human rights has transformed a domain traditionally allotted to constitutions—i.e., rights—into a transnational realm. The spread of constitutional adjudication and the proliferation of constitutional courts all over the world has also created a privileged judicial realm for the diffusion of legal arguments, which have been imitated for substantial or even 'diplomatic reasons', as David Law names them. Even administrative law is subject to certain uniformizing trends, as is demonstrated by the 'Global Administrative Law' project, which includes norms, principles, and institutions involving several states. It analyses what administrations are, beyond a merely domestic perspective, and takes into consideration the plethora of actors (international or supranational organizations and regional settings) that are exercising administrative tasks alongside the state.

Not only are all fields prone to comparison and circulation of models, but also all formants are involved, in both intra-formant (from legislator to legislator, from judge to judge) and extra-formant influence. Cross-imitations are frequent. In other words, legislators draw on pieces of legislation from other countries for inspiration, almost creating a kind of international community, in the words of Daphne Barak-Erez. Judgements and judicial interpretations or customs are also referred to when convenient. The same thing happens within courts, quoting foreign legal solutions, because they do not rely exclusively on previous judgements but also on different sources. Various jurisdictions throughout the world, for instance, quote scholarship in addition to foreign judgements. Latin American courts are an example of this. Swiss and Canadian judges even refer to PhD theses, and not only to established scholarship. The evolution of US law provides an additional example of this intersectoral circulation, as law-makers, judges, and legislators have relied upon continental European Civil Law sometimes even more than on British norms in order to build the American legal system, as H. Patrick Glenn has pointed out. The judicial and the scholarly formants were the protagonists, but still, in the 20th century the imitation went on—as is proven by the Uniform Commercial Code.

Facilitating elements

In the same way that language can be an obstacle to the circulation of legal solutions, it can also be a facilitator for studying and incorporating foreign norms. It is not by chance that Latin America follows Spanish, Portuguese, or French systems as a priority (in addition to US law, although for different reasons);

nor that English-speaking countries refer to each other more readily, even when they belong to different areas of the world (from the US to India, to Australia, or South Africa). In this respect, belonging to the same tradition is an asset since legal institutions are more comparable and more likely to respond to similar cultural/historical needs, like the British roots of the Common Law countries and the Commonwealth.

As explained in Chapter 2 concerning legal transplants, prestige and political/economic convenience also play a role in transforming a domestic legal solution into a 'model'. Supposedly prestigious systems with powerful courts, like that of Germany within Europe, are more likely to serve as sources of inspiration for others, especially for courts such as those of Central and Eastern Europe, which were designed by imitating the German example. The same applies to politically dominant countries within certain areas, like India in South-East Asia.

Additionally, economic efficiency can be pursued as a means to modernize and attract foreign capital, easing commercial relations and adapting national standards to those of investors' backgrounds. Further geopolitical and economic targets can be pursued through the expansion of regional and international trade arrangements, such as the US–Mexico–Canada Agreement (USMCA) 2020 after the North American Free Trade Agreement (NAFTA); or all of the EU's trade agreements with third-countries. The success of these agreements is facilitated by the achievement of a certain degree of legal homogeneity, which, at times, is required. Entry into the Southern Common Market— MERCOSUR, a regional organization comprising Argentina, Brazil, Paraguay, and Uruguay and later Venezuela—also implies the easing of access to other markets and the harmonization of domestic commercial legislations.

Trade and commerce, in contemporary times, involve a transnational dimension even outside such frameworks. More and more contracts bind partners from different countries, necessarily postulating the establishment of common ground. The implications of a *bona fide* (good faith) contract clause may vary under German, Canadian, or Chinese law, and defining its contours is essential to determine the contractual obligations of parties coming from different systems.

Again, political interests can be driving forces towards foreign models. The need to obey similar requirements to achieve a target is a powerful one. The example of the so-called 'Copenhagen criteria', i.e., the requirements to define whether a country is eligible to join the EU in terms of its respect for democracy and human rights, as well as having a market economy, suffices. The accession conditionality applied to potential new member states, before the enlargement of 2004, led to the circulation of norms and legal models to provide for this uniformity. Already in 1998, the European Community's Phare Programme provided financial and technical support to thirteen partner countries in Central and Eastern Europe, aiming to share best practices from member states with ten prospective members as well as supporting the transition to democracy and a market economy of three further countries. Similar mechanisms of conditionality have bridled African parliaments into regulating liberalizations or political decentralization within international development programmes.

Belonging to the EU (or other supranational organizations) by itself implies a certain level of legal convergence in the areas of domain of the organization. This explains why previous European measures are quoted and referred to when passing amendments in this respect. For example, German, Italian, Spanish, British, and Polish measures were quoted when the French parliament passed its latest law to raise the minimum age for pensions. The relatively frequent debates on electoral reforms in Italy also consider the plethora of European systems.

Digitalization and the spread of official websites, with databases available online in several languages, are additional facilitators for comparison in contemporary times. Parliaments, courts, and other institutions have official websites that often provide translations into English or another *lingua franca* in order to make norms and decisions available to a wider public. Of course, this cannot be applicable to traditions in which orality or customs prevail in law-making.

Networks involving courts, parliaments, and other institutions also foster dialogue and mutual exchange. Bilateral, trilateral, multilateral meetings or conferences of constitutional and supreme courts across the world are more and more frequent. Parliamentary associations, such as the Commonwealth Parliamentary Association, Inter-Parliamentary Union, Parliamentary Confederation of the Americas, and the National Conference of State Legislatures in the US, have provided excellent fora in which to exchange ideas.

In Europe, interparliamentary cooperation also relies upon digital means: notably, the Interparliamentary EU Information Exchange offers comparative models of transposition of directives, and the European Centre for Parliamentary Research and Documentation has become a community of parliamentary knowledge. The African Parliamentary Knowledge Network has aimed to improve the capacity and effectiveness of parliaments by providing a platform for sharing information between legislative bodies as well as improving the quality of legislation. Similarly, the Parlatino (Parlamento Latinoamericano y Caribeño), a regional permanent body established in 1987 and composed of the legislatures of Latin America and the Caribbean, counts within its mandate a push towards legislative harmonization and the drafting of 'model statutes'. Soft diplomacy, consisting in contacts and less formalized interactions among parliaments' staff and members of parliament from different countries, is an additional, effective tool for mutual exchange and learning.

The internal institutional setting can also facilitate imitations and consideration of comparative examples. Parliaments with units devoted to foreign and comparative law, courts with research divisions (like the Comparative Law Research Division in the Supreme Court of Argentina, the Czech Analytic Department established fifteen years ago, and the sub-unit of the Italian Constitutional Court devoted to comparative law) have an easier job when deciding to engage in legal comparison. Finally, the background and required expertise of the members of the corresponding courts are also important, with judges coming from academia usually more inclined towards comparative arguments.

Each country's expertise also plays a role in the likelihood of it becoming a model. When reforming laws on earthquakes, Japan or Chile come to mind; Spain or Denmark when regulating *in vitro* fertilization; the US or Germany when amending federal systems; and so on. Timing should not be undervalued either. The first system to regulate a new issue is the most likely to become a model for others. Think of the US Bankruptcy Reform Act of 1978, or the US Genetic Information Nondiscrimination Act of 2008. Pieces of legislation fostering gender equality, regulating same-sex marriage, or addressing pressing bioethical issues over the past years have become direct or indirect sources of inspiration for countries facing the same problem at a later date, in spite of the issues arising from transplants that were addressed in Chapter 2.

Education and improvement of critical skills

Comparative law contributes to the improvement of the education of lawyers and scholars not unlike the ways in which legal philosophy or general theory do. It represents an epistemological and methodological addition to their education. It helps broaden their understanding of the law, their comprehension of foreign realities, and the social dimension of legal rules. It entails an insightful intellectual exercise which allows scholars to improve their communication with colleagues from all over the world, while potentially enhancing their linguistic skills. In this respect, studies intersecting linguistics, translation, interpretation, and legal comparison lie at the core of comparative education, similarly to the analysis of the changing *lingua franca* within the transnational arena (from Latin, to French, to English).

Getting to know 'the law of the others' is also a powerful tool for grasping the peculiarities and the inner roots of one's own law. The discovery of foreign legal solutions allows you to put yours into perspective and to investigate the reasons for arrangements that you have taken for granted. History, politics, and geography may have determined a certain legal solution in one country and a completely different one in another, which may work just as well or even better. One example could be France, which has more than 35,000 municipalities, while Spain and Italy have approximately 8,000, for social, historical, and geographical reasons. Greece dramatically reduced its number of municipalities in 2010 through a dedicated plan. A French-educated expert in local government may take for granted that the legal system should provide for the preservation of the smallest municipalities and their distribution throughout the territory. A (legal) incursion into neighbouring countries may show that this is not the case and offer mechanisms to foster fusions and shared management of local functions. Not only similar cases, but also very distant cases or outlier examples can be of great help to understand the meaning and scope of legal concepts. The study of the Chinese *sui generis* constitution and constitutionalism, for instance, proves this, as Albert Chen has recently shown.

Comparative knowledge, combined with the consequent critical understanding of the law of the country, facilitates one of its most practical uses, namely the proposal of new laws or their amendment. This function has been called by Michael Bogdan working *de lege ferenda*, while judges often operate within a set of given norms, therefore, working *de lege lata*.

Legislative use

Legislators can make use of comparative legal solutions to copy, adapt, and amend foreign norms. And often not the particular norm, but rather the idea, the logic, behind legal solutions is what really influences others.

Empirical analysis shows that this process of imitation (or at least consideration of comparative law) takes place at different points in the legislative procedure. Comparative knowledge is inserted into the discussion in the corresponding committees or subcommittees (foreign affairs, economics and finance, environmental policies, etc.) through dedicated dossiers required by the members of parliament as well as through individual interventions of members of parliament in the debate who use them as arguments *quoad auctoritatem*, i.e., as opinions of an authority or a prestigious source which are used to support the main argument.

The role of the internal bodies of the legislative chambers and particularly of the committees dedicated to the thematic appraisal, discussion, and study of bills is paramount in this respect. They can collect materials of comparative legislation (as well as case law or scholarship) to extend the debate to foreign models. In Argentina, for instance, the parliament established a foreign law department within the directorate for parliamentary information, formalizing the practice existing in many legislatures. In France, an *exposé des motifs* and an *étude d'impact* are required, which often contain comparative elements endorsing the legislative choices.

Comparative references can be useful, particularly for comprehensive reforms and/or very current topics. For instance, to achieve the extensive reform of federal criminal law in the 1970s the US Senate collected comparative materials covering countries all over the world and arranged a hearing to ask scholars specific questions through a dedicated questionnaire (1972).

Coming to 'hot' topics at the time of legislative approval, the Canadian Environmental Protection Act (1999) drew inspiration from previous German regulations for the inclusion of new substance notification programmes. Experts were also consulted to explain the impact of European norms concerning the removal of toxic products, for example. Environmental protection is a significant example of the diffusion of models, not only from one domestic system to another or from an international regime to a national level but also in the opposite direction, that is, from the domestic to the international. Legal responses to environmental and climate change are particularly likely to be circulated as they address ubiquitous issues. Of course, all imitations in law still require an adaptation of the foreign norms, but less so than in other domains which are more context based.

Over the past ten years, a pressing issue has been how to accommodate religious minority groups within Western secular states. Domestic and international courts and legislators have been involved in the debate providing a set of interpretations of religious freedom and the displaying of religious symbols in public spaces. The well-known 2010 French law banning face coverings in public spaces relied on extensive comparative references, including existing norms in Austria, Germany, and the UK, Denmark's limitations on the use of *burqas* and *niqaab* in public, as well as measures discussed in the Netherlands with respect to the use of these coverings in schools. Most efforts were devoted to considering Belgium, which offered a precedent in having embedded a similar general prohibition in their legal system.

The 'model statutes' provided by the previously mentioned Parlatino are significant in terms of the topicality of certain issues. Tellingly, in 2022 a model statute to guarantee human rights when accessing information technologies and communication through the internet was published; as was one concerning remote working, which had become so popular during the pandemic emergency.

Even administrations less prone to using foreign law sometimes decide to do so. The UK Law Commission provides one interesting example in this respect. When studying the amendments to the insurance contract law a decade ago, it examined the rules on late payment of claims in Australia, the US, and Canada as well as those of China, Germany, Italy, and Spain, highlighting the degree of protection for the insured subject, and the shortcomings and advantages of each system.

Legislative comparison is not a recent process at all, as the circulation of models over time proves. For instance, the Chilean Civil Code of 1855, drafted by Andrés Bello by adapting the French Civil Code of 1804 and other laws such as the Spanish Siete Partidas to the 'country's peculiar circumstances', was later adopted in El Salvador, Ecuador, Venezuela, Nicaragua, Colombia, and Honduras, and it influenced the civil codes of Uruguay, Mexico, Guatemala, Costa Rica, and Paraguay.

Use in constituent processes

Democratic constitutions all over the world have recurrent, or at least comparable, content and language. They contain the core values and features of a polity. They define rights, the organization of powers, the political system, decentralization, the role of courts, among other aspects.

Particularly, constitutions adopted after the Second World War have become part of a growing circulation of models. In Europe in the 1970s, the drafters of the constitutions of Greece, Portugal, and Spain debated foreign constitutional clauses to imitate and/or reject or adapt them to their own context. The Spanish constitution is a significant example in this respect: the drafting of the equality clause and the definition of regional organization were expressly inspired by both the Italian and the German constitutions; the debate on direct democracy took into account the mechanisms already in place in Switzerland and the UK; and so on.

Constitutional design in the 1990s was also very much indebted to comparative law in Eastern Europe, especially with respect to the role of the state in the economy, as some states were shifting from a planned economy to liberal standards. A similar phenomenon occurred in Latin America as well. In fact, Latin American early constitutionalism was influenced by the US constitution (especially with respect to its presidential system) and the Spanish constitution of Cádiz from 1812. In the 20th century, the spread of social paradigms of states and the constitutional regulation of social, economic, and cultural rights made the Mexican constitution (1917), the Russian constitution (1918), the Weimar constitution (1919), and the Austrian constitution (1929) very appealing for those drafting new texts or reforming older ones. The displacement of dictatorial regimes in later processes of reform was subject to further influences. Several countries have hybridized their presidential arrangements by including mechanisms comparable to the no-confidence vote regulated in European parliamentary systems (Spain, Italy, Germany), or semi-presidential systems (France, Portugal). The constituent debates leading to the Brazilian constitution of 1988 weighed the pros and cons of presidentialism and parliamentarism by discussing existing regimes in America and Europe, to identify which model may best suit the country and reinforce political pluralism (presidentialism was later confirmed in the 1993 constitutional referendum). Also, the debate on rights and their social dimension in the 1991 Colombian constitution drew inspiration from comparative law. The founding fathers of the 1999 Venezuelan text prioritized Latin American systems while delving into other examples to select the most appropriate solutions (for instance, contesting the US model as far as the preamble was concerned).

African waves of constitutionalization show different patterns. The constitutions of independence were characterized by their application of Western standards without significant critical assessment of compatibility with the context they were to be received into. However, the later wave at the end of the 20th century showed a greater awareness of prior traditions. Conversely, in the early 2010s, the Arab Spring was activated by protests rising up against oppressive authoritarianism to achieve Western-style democratic political systems and improve the economic future. Knowledge of foreign systems and a wish to implement them in their own countries was one of the driving forces for the protesters, targets that are only partially reflected in the corresponding new constitutions.

Within the continent, South Africa represents a unique case. Already at the end of the 1980s the South African Law Reform Commission had studied forms of state, government, separation of powers and customs from European, Indian, American, and Australian systems. In spite of the relative scarcity of African references, the process differed from previous ones since the new leadership had the economic and intellectual resources to select the elements to imitate, and those to reject. For example, with respect to the territorial organization of powers, the constituent assembly took into consideration both decentralized and unitary models, and met with the German Prime Minister Kohl and some governors of the *Länder*, elaborating the tasks for parliamentary chambers.

More recently, the 2015 Nepalese constitution was influenced by the Indian system in aspects such as the establishment of a competitive multiparty democratic governance system, multiculturalism, multilingualism, and federalism. The comparative discussions that took place in the drafting of the Chilean constitution rejected in the 2022 plebiscite show that there is an ongoing process of circulation and adaptation of models. When debating the clauses regarding the relationship between domestic and international law, foreign mechanisms opening interpretation to international treaties were discussed, beginning with the Spanish case (Article 10 of the constitution). Similarly, economic principles of solidarity and the role of the state in the economy were contrasted with socio-liberal constitutional standards and norms on environmental protection. Comparatively, this process showed several peculiarities including: gender balance in the assembly, the representation of indigenous groups, or the recognition of international law as a limitation in the drafting of a new constitution. This example proves the truth of the expression 'circulation' applied to constitutional migrations of ideas, that is, a text that borrows might become a model. And this has happened to almost all texts over time.

Use in supranational and international law

Recent phenomena of aggregation among states have proved essential in increasing interest in comparative law and scholarship. These processes have two basic aims, namely, harmonization, i.e., making the norms of two or more countries more alike; and unification, i.e., setting common rules for all the member states. Drafting common rules can raise difficulties with respect to terminology and concepts, as well as in translations. Comparative methodology contributes to disentangling these.

In the initial phase, these experiments were enriched by the use of different models in their establishment. In this respect, the original European communities' legal framework represented an arena for legal transplants. Just a few examples suffice to grasp this. The preliminary reference to the Court of Justice, which is a mechanism whereby each domestic judge can ask for the decision on the interpretation or the validity of European norms, is based on the 'concrete control' that can be triggered in Italy by individual judges to obtain the Constitutional Court's decision on a matter. The establishment of the abovementioned Court of Justice's advocates general, who present 'opinions' on cases with impartiality and independence, is inspired by the French example of the *rapporteur public* acting before the French Council of State. Also, independent administrative authorities responding to the Anglo-Saxon conception of administration have been inserted into member states of continental Europe by hybridizing their model based on ministries.

Over time, substantive norms have been made more consistent in all the member states. Areas like consumer protection, product liability, or product's quality standards have been subject to Europeanization. European institutions use comparative information on domestic norms in order to provide harmonized or unified rules. Afterwards, domestic laws are repealed or amended so as to be coherent with the EU requirements. To avoid or at least reduce the possibility of different interpretations, the Court of Justice is the only institution in charge of providing the correct interpretation of EU norms. It also relies on legal comparison in its work. In particular, it is entitled to elaborate on the constitutional traditions common to the member states through legal comparison. In fact, fundamental rights can also result from these traditions as general principles of EU law. Additionally, in the current discussion on the threats to the common values of the EU enshrined in Article 2 of the Treaty on the European Union, the comparative construction of European law plays a major role. In 2022, in a known judgement on the 'rule of law conditionality' for the protection of the EU budget, the Court of Justice referred to a concept of rule of law shared by the member states in their constitutional traditions.

International law is connected to comparative law as well. Article 38 of the statute of the International Court of Justice mentioned the 'general principles of law recognized by civilized nations' as one of the sources it may employ. Even if the expression 'civilized nations' sounds more consistent with colonial times, the methodology of extrapolating norms from domestic systems is what comparative law often requires. Frequently also, customary public international law is inferred from the practices accepted and considered binding in different states.

The European Convention of Human Rights also refers to the law recognized by civilized nations (Article 7) and, more generally, it relies upon complex processes of mutual understanding and the setting of transnational standards. The European Court of Human Rights, in the application of the Convention, has also elaborated the consensus doctrine, which is based on the comparative assessment of the signatory states in order to identify the existence of shared interpretations of the rights. The corresponding international human rights court in the Americas, namely, the Inter-American Court of Human Rights, makes use of comparative law as well, referring to precedents by the equivalent European court, but also to domestic norms and judgements which can provide inspiration.

Private international law is another domain in which legal comparison is paramount, as was addressed in Chapter 4. It is applied in cases in which parties from different countries are present. States have their own sources in order to fix the criteria to decide which law will be applicable to each case (this is why private international law is, in reality, domestic law). For instance, a system may establish that a divorce between spouses from different countries must be decided by means of the law of the country where they live, where they got married, or where they have their property. As a consequence, the judge deciding the case may be obliged to apply norms from another legal system (i.e., that of the couple's country of residence, marriage, etc.), engaging in the difficulties of understanding and interpreting foreign law. Similarly, when foreign judgements have to be enforced in a third country, comparative law can be useful. This is the case for criminal international law and extraditions, in which domestic judges are entitled to decide whether the conditions under which the person was convicted and judged are not inconsistent with those of the requested state.

Use by courts

Over the past decades, one of the most popular and studied phenomena of circulation has been that among courts, under the label of 'judicial dialogue'. Courts use foreign references, international legal sources, and also scholarship to reinforce their argument, rather than as a proper foundation for the decision. The South African Constitutional Court is an exception in this respect, since the use of legal comparison by constitutional judges is regulated in the constitution. Section 39, paragraph 1, states that 'When interpreting the Bill of Rights, a court, tribunal or forum (a) must promote the values that underlie an open and democratic society based on human dignity, equality and freedom; (b) must consider international law; and (c) may consider foreign law'.

Constitutional and supreme courts are the ones that more frequently include in their judgements references to foreign and international law. The expertise of the justices, the special tasks allotted to these courts, and the relevance of the cases are only some of the factors explaining it. As happens with parliaments, (judicial) politics matters. Recently established courts are more prone to quote foreign precedents, especially by established courts, in order to legitimize their decisions. Courts in countries exiting dictatorships or authoritarian regimes may do the same to infuse content into the novel legal rules, embracing democratic values. On the contrary, established courts may be reluctant to turn to other courts' decisions as it could be seen as a *deminutio* of their prestige. Some courts have even been prohibited from referring to foreign sources, as in the case of the French Court of Cassation.

Comparative references can be found in different parts of judgements, namely, in the *ratio decidendi* (the main argument), the *obiter dicta* (the additional parts), or individual opinions in courts that allow for them. Depending on the location, the purpose changes—rarely is it the foundation of the decision; more often, it represents an *argumentum ad adiuvandum* (an additional argument in the reasoning) and even more frequently, it is an argument reinforcing the opinion of dissenting judges. Interestingly, in a few cases it is used as a counterargument, as an element of comparison with a legal solution that the court is not inclined to adopt.

Several scholars have engaged in classifications of how and why courts rely on comparative law. Ulrich Drobnig in the 1980s distinguished between cases in which the 'external' reference is optional (*freiwillige*) and where it is obligatory (*notwendige*), like in private international law. Basil Markesinis and Jorg Fedtke identified three categories: (a) courts counting on constitutional clauses obliging them to take it into account (only South Africa); (b) courts that adopt corrective decisions when the legislator has not yet followed social change (Germany in the wake of the Second World War); and (c) courts actually pushing the legal system towards novel solutions (US and Israel). From a more general perspective, Mads Andenas and Duncan Fairgrieve acknowledged seven targets for the recourse to foreign legal sources: (a) to support a rule or an outcome; (b) to fill a gap in the legal system or provide a solution when there are many; (c) to anticipate potential outcomes of a rule that is new in national law; (d) to restate or contest the universality of a rule; (e) to support the overruling of a precedent rule; (f) to help develop principles of domestic law; and (g) to solve issues in the application of international law. More recently, Giuseppe Franco Ferrari offered additional elements to contextualize these references, like the practice of citing just one country or several; the weight and effectiveness of the quotations; or the effects.

From a Western perspective, the interest in this issue was present for decades in Europe and was sparked again by the US Supreme Court's entry into the topic in the judgement *Lawrence v. Texas*

(2003), the landmark case which declared unconstitutional the criminal punishment of sodomy. The US debate exemplifies the dichotomy separating those in favour of using foreign experiences, and those in favour of defending the identity and self-standing of the legal system. The discussion between Justice Breyer and Justice Scalia presents two opposite ways of understanding constitutional interpretation and the role of judiciaries vis-à-vis globalization. The former believed in openness and mutual influences, while the latter advocated for an originalist exegesis of the constitution, based mainly on its understanding when it was passed. Therefore, foreign statutes, judicial decisions, and international law should not contribute to the construction of domestic judgements. Already in 1997, Scalia stated that 'comparative analysis is inappropriate in the task of interpreting a constitution' (*Printz v. United States*). That of comparative references is a recurring debate in the US Supreme Court, especially in important cases, such as the famous decision *Dobbs v. Jackson Women's Health Organization* (2022) which returned to individual member states the power to regulate abortion in all aspects not governed by federal law. Both the majority and the dissenters of the case relied upon comparative law to support their viewpoint.

The Common Law world, in general, is particularly inclined towards circulation of case law, due to the value of binding precedents and shared legal roots. Indian case law, by the Supreme Court and inferior jurisdictions, significantly relies on judgements, commentaries, and scholarly writings by authors of Common Law countries. Similarly, former British colonies in Africa like Ghana or Nigeria also quote British precedents, in addition to judgements issued in other Common Law jurisdictions.

As was recalled, a shared language also helps, as is the case for Latin America, where the linguistic, historical, and legal ties and similarities, as well as the common colonial European heritage and American influence, have led to the diffusion of foreign legal solutions and imitations. Latin American courts quote norms, judgements, and scholars, particularly as additional arguments that reinforce the reasoning. Often the US Supreme Court is present, but also internal Latin American circulation happens alongside a dialogue with Europe and beyond. The Federal Brazilian Supreme Court even labels paragraphs in the judgement as 'comparative law', as happened in relevant cases such as that relating to first-trimester abortion in 2016. The Argentinian Supreme Court's 1996 decision (*Nardelli*) on convictions *in absentia* quoted British, Italian, German, French, and US law, while the 2015 decision on hydration and nutrition as medical treatments referred to Italian, Indian, and French jurisprudence along the same lines, as well as cases by the European Court of Human Rights. When inaugurating a new line of jurisprudence in 2003, in order to elaborate upon constitutional adjudication of constitutional amendments, the Colombian Constitutional Court mentioned the Indian Supreme Court's 'basic structure doctrine'. For a long time, references were made mainly to Global North 'precedents' by non-Western courts or courts not belonging to the 'usual suspects'; recently, quotations running in the opposite direction have also been observed as well as an internal circulation of ideas within the Global South, as the last example shows.

Chapter 7
An evolving field

For most participants at the 1900 Paris Congress, comparative law consisted of enumerating similarities and differences between the legal systems of two or more states. At that time, enquiry typically focused on Common and Civil Law with a view to finding out how a country A and a country B—preferably 'grand' or 'parent' legal systems—dealt with the same practical situation. It was grounded in the analysis of written rules and formalized law, primarily statutory texts and judicial decisions.

Over time, less conventional forms of comparison made the discipline more flexible and diverse. This substantial redefinition necessitated an abandoning of its original limitations: Western and state laws as the conventional units of analysis, written rules as the sole legal sources, functionalism as the only possible methodology, and private law as the main field of study.

Comparative law widened out its field of enquiry to non-Western and non-state laws and rejected the idea of national legal systems as homogeneous entities. Adopting a plurality of methods and addressing traditionally overlooked topics and geographical areas, it expanded its understanding of law and also embraced greater interdisciplinarity: history, political science, linguistics, anthropology, ethnography, sociology, economics, computer science, and so on. It went beyond formal sources of law to look at any element contributing to social order, including unwritten sources and unofficial records.

Comparative law scholars began exploring distant cultures once deemed unsuited to analysis, studying sub-national and supranational laws, and contrasting contemporary laws with the legal systems of the past. As a result, a growing volume of studies are now dedicated to investigating non-state, non-territorial legal orders and alternative forms of normativity—aboriginal, religious, and chthonic laws, corporate rules, and even criminal organizations—and tracking their interaction. Even an in-depth account of a single legal system entails comparison when it focuses on those who live as foreigners within that system and see it from a different perspective: the suppressed and the marginalized, such as minorities and migrants. New labels have been coined for this: 'comparative international law', 'diachronic comparison', or 'minor comparison', among many others.

At least in part, this diversity mirrors the field's various aims. Comparative research can pursue theoretical or practical outcomes. It may serve the purpose of learning about foreign laws for the sake of knowledge and in order to study prototypical laws, the most popular ones or those deemed more deserving for some reason. At the same time, it can be seen as a powerful self-reflection tool, as looking at how others do things gives us something valuable to take back home. It is a way of 'going native' and seeing the world through the eyes of locals or testing a general hypothesis about the law empirically. It is instrumental in identifying global trends and recurring patterns from which to derive abstract models and contribute to general theory building. Comparative research can either encompass detailed examinations of a small number of cases or provide a statistical analysis of large data sets. It focuses on the trees or the forest and prioritizes depth or forgoes it for breadth. It tells us a little about a lot or offers a dense description of just one jurisdiction. It may show a preference for the 'usual suspects' or for 'radically different' cultures, take the most travelled roads, or explore uncharted terrain.

Admittedly, this diversity is the main reason for the sector's perpetual crisis and eternal search for disciplinary definition. Even to its adepts, comparative law can often be an enigmatic and elusive subject. This absence of clarity raises the critical question of where to fix the boundaries and whether the general heading can incorporate the broadening scope of comparative endeavours. The field's enlargement makes comparative law ubiquitous, overlapping with other legal and non-legal disciplines. Some are now arguing for the end of the discipline, while others prefer to bring all the variants under a single 'big tent'. The extraordinary diversity of laws, topics, sources, methods, and aims tends to invoke accusations of cherry-picking where there is any comparative inquiry, with the immense volume of material potentially needing digesting and the countless possible choices to be made.

Such criticisms should be taken seriously. The pursuit of a common canon of knowledge with an internal coherence remains a fundamental challenge for the discipline. At the same time, the limitations of each approach and any accusations of arbitrariness are, to a considerable extent, more about a call to do a good job than a criticism of the discipline *per se*. As Tom Ginsburg once suggested, comparativists are like the blind men in the famous Buddhist tale who try to describe an elephant by touching portions of it. Any individual attempting to do the job alone is doomed to failure. It is only by combining our manifold and divergent views that we can get the bigger picture. The most diverse currents of scholarship can contribute to getting a sense of the elephant as long as they are explicit about their aims, goals, and the scope of their enquiry, and reflect these choices in a clear methodology, research design, and case selection.

In the absence of a dominant approach to the discipline, no magic bullet is likely to end this heterogeneity. The future will possibly bring even more diversity and flexibility. This lack of clarity in approach to the field is a source of concern but it also represents a beneficial force. Uncertainties about the future of the academic discipline should be reckoned with and discussed. In the meantime, we can comfort ourselves by looking at the extraordinary body of scholarship that has been crafted over the course of a century and praise the practice of comparative law for the richness and diversity it brings to the study of law.

References and further reading

Chapter 1: What is comparative law?

D. Berg-Schlosser, 'Comparative Studies: Method and Design', in N.J. Smelser and P.B. Baltes (eds), *International Encyclopedia of the Social & Behavioral Sciences* (Elsevier, 2001).

M. Bussani, 'Comparative Law beyond the Trap of Western Positivism', in I.C. Tong, and S. Mancuso (eds), *New Frontiers of Comparative Law* (Lexis-Nexis, 2013).

M. Bussani and U. Mattei (eds), *The Cambridge Companion to Comparative Law* (Cambridge University Press, 2012).

D.S. Clark, 'Nothing New in 2000? Comparative Law in 1900 and Today', 75 *Tulane Law Review* 871 (2001).

P. De Cruz, *Comparative Law in a Changing World* (Routledge, 2007, 3rd edn).

B. Fauvarque-Cosson, 'Development of Comparative Law in France', in M. Reimann and R. Zimmermann (eds), *The Oxford Handbook of Comparative Law* (Oxford University Press, 2019, 2nd edn).

G. Frankenberg, 'Critical Comparisons: Re-thinking Comparative Law', 26 *Harvard Law Review* 411 (1985).

G. Frankenberg, *Comparative Constitutional Studies: Between Magic and Deceit* (Edward Elgar, 2019).

S. Gordon, *When Asia Was the World: Traveling Merchants, Scholars, Warriors, and Monks Who Created the 'Riches of the East'* (Da Capo Press, 2008).

R. Hirschl, *Comparative Matters: The Renaissance of Comparative Constitutional Law* (Oxford University Press, 2014).

U. Kischel, *Comparative Law* (Oxford University Press, 2019).

P. Legrand and R. Munday (eds), *Comparative Legal Studies: Traditions and Transitions* (Cambridge University Press, 2003).

L. Nader, *What the Rest Think of the West: Since 600 AD* (University of California Press, 2015).

L. Pegoraro and A. Rinella, *Derecho constitucional comparado. La ciencia y el método* (Astrea, 2016).

M. Reimann, 'Comparative Law and Neighbouring Disciplines', in M. Bussani and U. Mattei (eds), *The Cambridge Companion to Comparative Law* (Cambridge University Press, 2012).

M. Reimann and R. Zimmermann (eds), *The Oxford Handbook of Comparative Law* (Oxford University Press, 2019, 2nd edn).

A. Riles (ed.), *Rethinking the Masters of Comparative Law* (Hart, 2001).

T. Ruskola, *Legal Orientalism: China, the United States, and Modern Law* (Harvard University Press, 2013).

R. Sacco, 'One Hundred Years of Comparative Law', 75 *Tulane Law Review* 1159 (2001).

Chapter 2: Classifying legal systems

G.F. Bell, 'The Civil Law, the Common Law, and the English Language—Challenges and Opportunities in Asia', 14 *Asian Journal of Comparative Law* 29 (2019).

D. Berkowitz, K. Pistor, and J.F. Richard, 'The Transplant Effect', 51 *American Journal of Comparative Law* 163 (2003).

M. Chiba, *Legal Pluralism: Towards a General Theory Through Japanese Legal Culture* (Tokai University Press, 1989).

R. Cotterrell, *Law, Culture and Society: Legal Ideas in the Mirror of Social Theory* (Routledge, 2006).

R. David, *Les grands systèmes de droit contemporains* (Dalloz, 1964).

R. David, C. Jauffret-Spinosi, and M. Goré, *Les grands systemes de droit contemporains* (Dalloz, 2016, 12th edn).

B. de Sousa Santos, *Epistemologies of the South: Justice against Epistemicide* (Routledge, 2014).

R. Dixon and D. Landau, *Abusive Constitutional Borrowing: Liberal Globalization and the Subversion of Liberal Democracy* (Oxford University Press, 2021).

G. Frankenberg, 'Constitutional Transfer: The IKEA Theory Revisited', 8 *International Journal of Constitutional Law* 563 (2010).

G. Frankenberg, *Order from Transfer: Comparative Constitutional Design and Legal Culture* (Edward Elgar, 2013).

H.P. Glenn, *Legal Traditions of the World* (Oxford University Press, 2014, 5th edn).

T.S. Goldbach, 'Instrumentalizing the Expressive: Transplanting Sentencing Circles into the Canadian Criminal Trial', 25 *Transnational Law & Contemporary Problems* 61 (2015).

M. Graziadei, 'Comparative Law, Transplants, and Receptions', in M. Reimann and R. Zimmermann (eds), *The Oxford Handbook of Comparative Law* (Oxford University Press, 2019, 2nd edn).

S. Grundmann, H. Micklitz, and M. Renner, *New Private Law Theory. A Pluralist Approach* (Cambridge University Press, 2021).

J. Husa, 'Classification of Legal Families Today: Is It Time for a Memorial Hymn?', 56 *Revue Internationale de Droit Comparé* 11 (2004).

S. Kalantry, 'Reverse Legal Transplants', 99 *North Carolina Law Review* 49 (2020).

M. Langer, 'Revolution in Latin America Criminal Procedure: Diffusion of Legal Ideas from the Periphery', 55 *American Journal of Comparative Law* 617 (2007).

M. Langer, 'From Legal Transplants to Legal Translations: The Globalization of Plea Bargaining and the Americanization Thesis in Criminal Procedure', 45 *Harvard International Law Journal* 1 (2004).

P. Legrand, 'The Impossibility of Legal Transplants', 4 *Maastricht Journal of European and Comparative Law* 111 (1997).

U. Mattei, 'Three Patterns of Law: Taxonomy and Change in the World's Legal Systems', 45 *American Journal of Comparative Law* 5 (1997).

W. Menski, *Comparative Law in a Global Context: The Legal Systems of Asia and Africa* (Cambridge University Press, 2006, 2nd edn).

W. Menski, *Hindu Law: Beyond Tradition and Modernity* (Oxford University Press, 2003).

W. Menski, 'Muslim Law in Britain', 62 *Journal of Asian and African Studies* 127 (2001).

F. Nicola, 'The Global Diffusion of U.S. Legal Thought: Changing Influence, National Security and Legal Education in Crisis', in C. Crawford and D. Bonilla Maldonado (eds), *Constitutionalism in the Americas* (Edward Elgar, 2018).

H.W. Okoth-Ogendo, 'Constitutions without Constitutionalism', in D. Greenberg, S.N. Katz, M.B. Oliviero, and S.C. Wheatley (eds), *Constitutions and Democracy: Transitions in the Contemporary World* (Oxford University Press, 1993).

E. Örücü, *The Enigma of Comparative Law: Variations on a Theme for the Twenty-First Century* (Martinus Nijhoff Publishers, 2004).

E. Örücü, 'Family Trees for Legal Systems: Towards a Contemporary Approach', in M. Van Hoecke (ed.), *Epistemology and Methodology of Comparative Law* (Hart Publishing, 2004).

V.V. Palmer, 'Mixed Legal Systems', in M. Bussani and U. Mattei (eds), *The Cambridge Companion to Comparative Law* (Cambridge University Press, 2012).

M. Pargendler, 'The Rise and Decline of Legal Families', 60 *American Journal of Comparative Law* 1043 (2012).

M. Reimann (ed.), *The Reception of Continental Ideas in the Common Law World 1820–1920* (Duncker & Humblot Gmbh, 1993).

A. Santos and D.M. Trubek (eds), *The New Law and Economic Development: A Critical Appraisal* (Cambridge University Press, 2006).

G. Sauser-Hall, *Fonction and méthode du droit comparé* (Kundig, 1913).

P. Shah, 'Globalisation and the Challenge of Asian Legal Transplants in Europe', *Singapore Journal of Legal Studies* 348 (2005).

M. Siems, 'The Power of Comparative Law: What Type of Units Can Comparative Law Compare?', 67 *American Journal of Comparative Law* 861 (2019).

J.M. Smits (ed.), *Elgar Encyclopedia of Comparative Law* (Edward Elgar, 2006).

I. Szabó and Z. Péteri (eds), *A Socialist Approach to Comparative Law* (Sijthoff, 1977).

G. Teubner, 'Legal Irritants: Good Faith in British Law or How Unifying Law Ends Up in New Divergences', 61 *The Modern Law Review* 11 (1998).

W. Twining, 'Comparative Law and Legal Theory: The Country and Western Tradition', in I. Edge (ed.), *Comparative Law in Global Perspective* (Brill, 2001).

S. Vogenauer, 'Common Law', in J. Basedow, K. Hopt, and R. Zimmermann (eds), *The Oxford Handbook on European Private Law* (Oxford University Press, 2012).

A. Watson, *Legal Transplants: An Approach to Comparative Law* (University of Virginia, 1974, 1st edn; University of Georgia Press, 1993, 2nd edn).

J.H. Wigmore, *Kaleidoscope of Justice: Containing Authentic Accounts of Trial Scenes from All Times and Climes* (Washington Law Book Co., 1941).

K. Zweigert and H. Kötz, *Introduction to Comparative Law* (North-Holland Pub. Co., 1977).

Chapter 3: Legal traditions

U. Baxi, 'The Colonialist Heritage', in P. Legrand and R. Munday (eds), *Comparative Legal Studies: Traditions and Transitions* (Cambridge University Press, 2003).

H.J. Berman, *Law and Revolution: The Formation of the Western Legal Tradition* (Harvard University Press, 1983).

T. Duve, 'Legal Traditions: A Dialogue between Comparative Law and Comparative Legal History', 6 *Comparative Legal History* 15 (2018).

O. Farahat, *The Foundation of Norms in Islamic Jurisprudence and Theology* (Cambridge University Press, 2019).

G. Gagnon, 'American Indian Law: A Discourse on Chthonic Law', 89 *North Dakota Law Review* 29 (2013).

M.A. Glendon, P. Carozza, and C. Picker, *Comparative Legal Traditions in a Nutshell* (West Academic Publishing, 2016, 4th edn).

H.P. Glenn, *Legal Traditions of the World* (Oxford University Press, 2014, 5th edn).

H.P. Glenn, 'Comparative Legal Families and Comparative Legal Traditions', in M. Reimann and R. Zimmermann (eds), *The Oxford Handbook of Comparative Law* (Oxford University Press, 2019, 2nd edn).

E. Goldsmith, *The Way: An Ecological World View* (Rider, 1992).

C. Imber, *Ebu's-Su'Ud: The Islamic Legal Tradition* (Edinburgh University Press, 1997).

J. Jany, *Legal Traditions in Asia: History, Concepts and Laws* (Springer, 2020).

U. Kischel, *Comparative Law* (Oxford University Press, 2019).

S. Mancuso and C.M. Fombad (eds), *Comparative Law in Africa: Methodologies and Concepts* (Juta and Company, 2015).

W. Menski, *Hindu Law: Beyond Tradition and Modernity* (Oxford University Press, 2003).

W. Menski, *Comparative Law in a Global Context: The Legal Systems of Asia and Africa* (Cambridge University Press, 2006, 2nd edn).

J.H. Merryman, *The Civil Law Tradition: An Introduction to the Legal Systems of Western Europe and Latin America* (Stanford University Press, 1969).

G. Mousourakis, *Comparative Law and Legal Traditions: Historical and Contemporary Perspectives* (Springer, 2019).

M. Nicolini, *Legal Geography: Comparative Law and the Production of Space* (Springer, 2022).

E. Örücü, 'Comparatists and Extraordinary Places', in P. Legrand and R. Munday (eds), *Comparative Legal Studies: Traditions and Transitions* (Cambridge University Press, 2003).

L. Pegoraro and A. Rinella, *Sistemi costituzionali* (Giappichelli, 2020).

F. Pollock and F.W. Maitland, *The History of English Law before the Time of Edward I* (Cambridge University Press, 1898, 2nd edn).

D. Trubek and M. Galanter, 'Scholars in Self-Estrangement: Some Reflections in the Crisis in Law and Development Studies in the United States', 4 *Wisconsin Law Review* 1062 (1974).

N. Zeineddine, *Die Methodik der islamischen Jurisprudenz. Uṣūl al-Fiqh* (Nomos, 2019).

Chapter 4: Methods and approaches

M. Adams and D. Heirbaut (eds), *The Method and Culture of Comparative Law—Essays in Honour of Mark Van Hoecke* (Hart Publishing, 2015).

J. Bell, 'Legal Research and the Distinctiveness of Comparative Law', in M.V. Hoecke (ed.), *Methodologies of Legal Research: What Kind of Method for What Kind of Discipline?* (Hart Publishing, 2011).

F. Bignami, 'Methodologies of Comparative Constitutional Law: Functional Approach', in *The Max Planck Encyclopedia of Comparative Constitutional Law* (2021).

M. Bussani and U. Mattei, 'The Common Core Approach to European Private Law', 3 *Columbia Journal of European Law* 339 (1997).

O.G. Chase, 'Legal Procedure and National Cultures', 5 *Cardozo Journal of International & Comparative Law* 1 (1987).

H.E. Chodosh, 'Comparing Comparisons: In Search of Methodology', 84 *Iowa Law Review* 1025 (1999).

M.R. Damaška, *The Faces of Justice and State Authority* (Yale University Press, 1986).

A. di Robilant, 'Big Questions Comparative Law', 96 *Boston University Law Review* 1325 (2016).

M. Dyson, 'Comparative Legal History: Methodology for Morphology', in O Moréteau, A. Masferrer, and K.A. Modéer (eds), *Edward Elgar Handbook of Comparative Legal History* (Edward Elgar, 2019).

W. Ewald, 'Comparative Jurisprudence (I): What Was it Like to Try a Rat?', 113 *University of Pennsylvania Law Review* 1889 (1995).

W. Ewald, 'Comparative Jurisprudence (II): What Was it Like to Try a Rat?', 43 *American Journal of Comparative Law* 489 (1995).

G.P. Fletcher, 'Comparative Law as a Subversive Discipline', 46, *American Journal of Comparative Law* 683 (1998).

G. Frankenberg, 'Comparing Constitutions: Ideas, Ideals, and Ideology—Toward a Layered Narrative', 4 *International Journal of Constitutional Law* 439 (2006).

D.J. Gerber, 'Method, Community and Comparative Law: An Encounter with Complexity Science', 16 *Roger Williams University Law Review* 110 (2011).

J. Gordley, 'The Functional Method', in P.G. Monateri (ed.), *Methods of Comparative Law* (Edward Elgar, 2012).

M. Graziadei, 'The Functionalist Heritage', in P. Legrand and R. Munday (eds), *Comparative Legal Studies: Traditions and Transitions* (Cambridge University Press, 2003).

V. Grosswald Curran, 'Cultural Immersion, Difference and Categories in U.S. Comparative Law', 46 *American Journal of Comparative Law* 43 (1998).

H.C. Gutteridge, *Comparative Law: An Introduction to the Comparative Method of Legal Study and Research* (Cambridge University Press, 1946).

J. Husa, 'Farewell to Functionalism or Methodological Tolerance?', 67 *Rabels Zeitschrift für ausländisches und internationales Privatrecht* 419 (2003).

O. Kahn-Freund, 'Comparative Law as an Academic Subject', 82 *Law Quarterly Review* 40 (1966).

R. La Porta et al., 'The Economic Consequences of Legal Origins', 46 *Journal of Economic Literature* 285 (2008).

J. Langbein, 'The German Advantage in Civil Procedure', 52 *University of Chicago Law Review* 825 (1985).

M. de S.-O.-l'E. Lasser, *Judicial Deliberations: A Comparative Analysis of Transparency and Legitimacy* (Oxford University Press, 2009).

P. Legrand, 'European Legal Systems Are Not Converging', 45 *The International & Comparative Law Quarterly* 52 (1996).

P. Legrand, 'Questions à Rodolfo Sacco', 4 *Revue Internationale de Droit Comparé* 943 (1995).

B. Markesinis, 'Comparative Law. A Subject in Search of an Audience', 53 *The Modern Law Review* 1 (1990).

R. Michaels, 'The Functional Method of Comparative Law', in
M. Reimann and R. Zimmermann (eds), *The Oxford Handbook of
Comparative Law* (Oxford University Press, 2019, 2nd edn).

P.G. Monateri (ed.), *Methods of Comparative Law* (Edward
Elgar, 2012).

S. Munshi, '"You Will See My Family Became So American": Toward a
Minor Comparativism', 63 *American Journal of Comparative Law*
655 (2015).

R. Pound, 'Comparative Law in Space and Time', 4 *American Journal
of Comparative Law* 70 (1955).

B. Pozzo, 'Comparative Law and Language', in M. Bussani and
U. Mattei (eds), *The Cambridge Companion to Comparative Law*
(Cambridge University Press, 2012).

E. Rabel, 'Das Problem der Qualifikation', 5 *RabelsZ* 241 (1931).

M. Reimann, 'The Progress and Failure of Comparative Law in the
Second Half of the Twentieth Century', 50 *American Journal of
Comparative Law* 671 (2003).

R. Sacco, 'Legal Formants: A Dynamic Approach to Comparative Law',
39 *American Journal of Comparative Law* 1 and 343 (1991).

G. Samuel, *An Introduction to Comparative Law and Method* (Hart
Publishing, 2014).

R.B. Schlesinger (ed.), *Formation of Contracts, A Study of the Common
Core of Legal Systems* (Dobbs, 1968).

S.C. Symeonides, *Codifying Choice of Law Around the World: An
International Comparative Analysis* (Oxford University Press, 2014).

M. van Hoecke (ed), *Epistemology and Methodology of Comparative
Law* (Hart Publishing, 2004).

S. Vogenauer, 'Sources of Law and Legal Method in Comparative Law',
in M. Reimann and R. Zimmermann (eds), *The Oxford Handbook
of Comparative Law* (Oxford University Press, 2019, 2nd edn).

F. Werro, 'Preface. What We Write About When We Write About
Comparative Law: Pierre Legrand's Critique in Discussion', 65
American Journal of Comparative Law (2017).

J.Q. Whitman, 'The Two Western Cultures of Privacy: Dignity Versus
Liberty', 113 *Yale Law Journal* 1151 (2004).

Chapter 5: Sameness and difference

L. Abu-Odeh, 'The Politics of (Mis)Recognition: Islamic Law
Pedagogy in American Academia', 52 *American Journal of
Comparative Law* 789 (2004).

M. Ancel, *Utilité et méthodes du droit comparé. Eléments d'introduction générale à l'étude comparative des droits* (Ides et Calendes, 1971).

D. Bonilla Maldonado, *Legal Barbarians: Identity, Modern Comparative Law and the Global South* (Cambridge University Press, 2021).

D.S. Clark, 'Nothing New in 2000? Comparative Law in 1900 and Today', 75 *Tulane Law Review* 871 (2001).

D.C. Clarke, 'Anti Anti-Orientalism, or Is Chinese Law Different?', 68 *American Journal of Comparative Law* 55 (2020).

V. Corcodel, *Modern Law and Otherness: The Dynamics of Inclusion and Exclusion in Comparative Legal Thought* (Edward Elgar, 2019).

V. Curran, 'Romantic Common Law, Enlightened Civil Law: Legal Uniformity and the Homogenization of the European Union', 7 *Columbia Journal of European Law* 63 (2001).

P. Dann, M. Riegner, and M. Bönnemann (eds), *The Global South and Comparative Constitutional Law* (Oxford University Press, 2020).

G. Dannemann, 'Comparative Law: Study of Similarities or Differences?', in M. Reimann and R. Zimmermann (eds), *The Oxford Handbook of Comparative Law* (Oxford University Press, 2019, 2nd edn).

H. Dedek, 'The Tradition of Comparative Law: Comparison and Its Colonial Legacy', in M. Siems and P.J. Yap (eds), *The Cambridge Handbook of Comparative Law* (Cambridge University Press, forthcoming).

J.L. Esquirol, 'The Fictions of Latin American Law (Part I)', 1997 *Utah Law Review* 425 (1997).

E. Grande, 'Hegemonic Human Rights and African Resistance: Female Circumcision in a Broader Comparative Perspective', 4 *Global Jurist* 3 (2004).

Da. Kennedy, 'The Methods and the Politics', in P. Legrand and R. Munday (eds), *Comparative Legal Studies: Traditions and Transitions* (Cambridge University Press, 2003).

Du. Kennedy, 'Political Ideology and Comparative Law', in M. Bussani and U. Mattei (eds), *The Cambridge Companion to Comparative Law* (Cambridge University Press, 2012).

M. de S.-O.-l'E. Lasser, 'Judicial (Self-)Portraits: Judicial Discourse in the French Legal System', 104 *Yale Law Journal* 1325 (1995).

P. Legrand, 'The Same and the Different', in P. Legrand and R. Munday (eds), *Comparative Legal Studies: Traditions and Transitions* (Cambridge University Press, 2003).

P. Legrand, 'John Henry Merryman and Comparative Legal Studies: A Dialogue', 47 *American Journal of Comparative Law* 3 (1999).

B. Markesinis, 'The Destructive and Constructive Role of the Comparative Lawyer', 57 *Rabels Zeitschrift für ausländisches und internationales Privatrecht* 438 (1993).

H. Muir-Watt, 'Further Terrains for Subversive Comparison: The Field of Global Governance and the Public, Private Divide', in P.G. Monateri (ed.), *Methods of Comparative Law* (Edward Elgar, 2012).

S. Munshi, 'Comparative Law and Decolonizing Critique', 65 *American Journal of Comparative Law* 207 (2017).

R. Sacco, 'Diversity and Uniformity in the Law', 49 *American Journal of Comparative Law* 179 (2001).

E. Said, *Culture and Imperialism* (Alfred A. Knopf, 1993).

L. Salaymeh and R. Michaels, 'Decolonial Comparative Law: A Conceptual Beginning', 86 *Rabels Zeitschrift für ausländisches und internationales Privatrecht* 166 (2022).

G. Samuel, 'All That Heaven Allows: Are Transnational Codes a "Scientific Truth" or Are They Just a Form of Elegant "Pastiche"?', in P.G. Monateri (ed.), *Methods of Comparative Law* (Edward Elgar, 2012).

R.B. Schlesinger, U. Mattei, T. Ruskola, and A. Gidi, *Schlesinger's Comparative Law* (Foundation Press, 2009, 7th edn).

A. Von Mehren, 'The Significance of Cultural and Legal Diversity for International Transactions', in E. von Caemmerer, S. Mentschikoff, and K. Zweigert (eds) *Ius Privatum Gentium. Festschriftfir Max Rheinstein*, vol. 1 (Mohr Siebeck, 1969).

A. Watson, *The Making of the Civil Law* (Harvard University Press, 1981).

J.Q. Whitman, 'The Neo-Romantic Turn', in P. Legrand and R. Munday (eds), *Comparative Legal Studies: Traditions and Transitions* (Cambridge University Press, 2003).

H.-E. Yntema, 'Comparative Legal Research, Some Remarks on "Looking Out of the Cave"', 54 *Michigan Law Review* 899 (1956).

Chapter 6: What for? The uses of comparative law

G. Ajani, 'By Chance and By Prestige: Legal Transplants in Russia and Eastern Europe', 43 *American Journal of Comparative Law* 93 (1995).

M. Andenas and D. Fairgrieve (eds), *Courts and Comparative Law* (Oxford University Press, 2015).

D. Barak-Erez, 'An International Community of Legislatures?', in R.W. Bauman and T. Kahana (eds), *The Least Examined Branch: The Role of Legislatures in the Constitutional State* (Cambridge University Press, 2009).

M. Bogdan, *Concise Introduction to Comparative Law* (Europa Law Publishing, 2012).

A.H.Y. Chen, 'Constitutions and Constitutionalism: China', in D.S. Law (ed.), *Constitutionalism in Context* (Cambridge University Press, 2022).

U. Drobnig, 'Die Nutzung der Rechtsvergleichung in der deutschen Rechtsbesprechung', 50 *Rabels Zeitschrift für ausländisches und internationales Privatrecht* 610 (1986).

U. Drobnig and S. van Erp (eds), *The Use of Comparative Law by Courts* (Kluwer Law International, 1999).

G.F. Ferrari (ed.), *Judicial Cosmopolitanism: The Use of Foreign Law in Contemporary Constitutional Systems* (Brill, 2019).

G.P. Fletcher, 'Comparative Law as a Subversive Discipline', 46 *American Journal of Comparative Law* 683 (1998).

H.P. Glenn, 'The Nationalist Heritage', P. Legrand and R. Munday (eds), *Comparative Legal Studies: Traditions and Transitions* (Cambridge University Press, 2003).

T. Groppi and M.-C. Ponthoreau (eds), *The Use of Foreign Precedents by Constitutional Judges* (Hart, 2013).

C. Hübner Mendes, R. Gargarella, and S. Guidi (eds), *The Oxford Handbook of Constitutional Law in Latin America* (Oxford University Press, 2022).

J. Husa, 'Turning the Curriculum Upside Down: Comparative Law as an Educational Tool for Constructing the Pluralistic Legal Mind', 10 *German Law Journal* 913 (2009).

V. Jackson, *Constitutional Engagement in a Transnational Era* (Oxford University Press, 2010).

O. Kahn-Freund, 'On Uses and Misuses of Comparative Law', 37 *The Modern Law Review* 1 (1974).

D.S. Law, 'Judicial Comparativism and Judicial Diplomacy', 163 *University of Pennsylvania Law Review* 4, 2015.

B.S. Markesinis and J. Fedtke, *Judicial Recourse to Foreign Law: A New Source of Inspiration?* (Routledge, 2006).

B.S. Markesinis and J. Fedtke, *Engaging with Foreign Law* (Hart, 2009).

L. Pegoraro and G.A. Figueroa Mejía, *Profesores y Jueces. Influjos de la doctrina en la jurisprudencia constitucional de Iberoamérica* (Centro de Estudios Constitucionales, 2016).

L. Scaffardi (ed.), *Parlamenti in dialogo. L'uso della comparazione nella funzione legislativa* (Jovene, 2011).

Chapter 7: An evolving field

T. Ginsburg, 'The State of the Field', in D.S. Law (ed.), *Constitutionalism in Context* (Cambridge University Press, 2022).

H.P. Glenn, 'The Aims of Comparative Law', in J.M. Smits (ed.), *Elgar Encyclopedia of Comparative Law* (Edward Elgar, 2006).

M. Grellette and C. Valcke, 'Comparative Law and Legal Diversity—Theorising about the Edges of Law', 5 *Transnational Legal Theory* 557 (2014).

D.S. Law, *Constitutionalism in Context* (Cambridge University Press, 2022).

S. Munshi, '"You Will See My Family Became So American": Toward a Minor Comparativism', 63 *American Journal of Comparative Law* 655 (2015).

E. Örücü, *The Enigma of Comparative Law: Variations on a Theme for the Twenty-First Century* (Martinus Nijhoff Publishers, 2004).

M. Siems, 'New Directions in Comparative Law', in M. Reimann and R. Zimmermann (eds), *The Oxford Handbook of Comparative Law* (Oxford University Press, 2019, 2nd edn)

F. Werro, 'Notes on the Purpose and Aims of Comparative Law', 75 *Tulane Law Review* 1225 (2001).

Index

For the benefit of digital users, indexed terms that span two pages (e.g., 52–53) may, on occasion, appear on only one of those pages.

A

abusive borrowing 34
Angrezi dharma 36
Angrezi shariat 36
animal trials 79–81
apple and orange comparison 92
argument *quoad auctoritatem* 115
argumentum *ad adiuvandum* 123–4

B

binding precedent see *stare decisis*

C

case (or factual) approach 72–3
civil law 21–2, 57–60, 94–6
classification 17, 20–8, 113–14
codification 21–2, 58
colonization 40–5
common law 21–3, 94–5
comparative linguistics 5–6
comparative religion 6
constituent process 117–20

constitutional adjudication 123
contrastive comparison 93, 101–3
Cornell Project *see* case (or factual) approach
cultural immersion 76–9

D

'distinguishing' 56
Doing Business Report 87–8

F

Fiqh 47–8
First International Congress of Comparative Law 2–3
foreign law 3–4, 13–15
functionalism 69–72, 76–9, 84–90, 96–8, 102

G

Global North 105–6
Global South 106, 125–6
glossators 47–8

H

harmonization 7–8, 89, 120
Hindu law *see* legal traditions:
    Hindu tradition
hybridity 28, 36

I

integrative comparison 93
interparliamentary cooperation 112
ius commune 18, 21–2, 57

J

Jewish law *see* legal traditions:
    Talmudic tradition
jury 54–5

L

language 69–70, 78–9, 109–10,
    125–6
law in action, law in
    books 33
law-making 115–17
legal change 29–35
legal families 19–27, 38, 93–6
legal formants 73–6
legal irritants 35
legal origins 85–8
legal traditions 27–8
    African traditions 43–5
    chthonic traditions 40–3
    Confucian tradition 52–3
    civil law tradition *see* civil law
    common law tradition
        see common law
    Hindu tradition 49–52
    Islamic tradition 47–9
    oral traditions 40–5
    religious traditions 45–9
    Talmudic tradition 38–9, 45–8,
        50, 61–5
        traditions of duties 49–53
        Western traditions 54–60, 94–5
legal transplants 30–7, 98–9
li 52–3

M

mirror theory of law 31–2

O

'overruling' 56

P

pluralism 27–8
positivism 39, 68, 73–4, 76–7, 89
postcolonial critique 104–6
praesumptio similitudinis
    97–8, 102

Q

quantitative comparative
    law 85–8

R

Roman law 21–2, 57

S

Sharia 47
sources of law 73–4
Soviet law 23–4, 95–6
stare decisis 18–19, 39

T

Talmudic tradition *see* legal
    traditions: Talmudic tradition
taxonomy 19–21, 25–7, 33, 78–9,
    93–6; *see also* classification

Torah 45-6
translation 69, 78-9, 83, 120

U

unification 99-101

V

Vedas 51

W

writ or form of action 54

AMERICAN POLITICAL PARTIES AND ELECTIONS
A Very Short Introduction
Sandy L. Maisel

Few Americans and even fewer citizens of other nations understand the electoral process in the United States. Still fewer understand the role played by political parties in the electoral process or the ironies within the system. Participation in elections in the United States is much lower than in the vast majority of mature democracies. Perhaps this is because of the lack of competition in a country where only two parties have a true chance of winning, despite the fact that a large number of citizens claim allegiance to neither and think badly of both. Studying these factors, you begin to get a very clear picture indeed of the problems that underlay this much trumpeted electoral system.

ENGLISH LITERATURE
A Very Short Introduction
Jonathan Bate

Sweeping across two millennia and every literary genre, acclaimed scholar and biographer Jonathan Bate provides a dazzling introduction to English Literature. The focus is wide, shifting from the birth of the novel and the brilliance of English comedy to the deep Englishness of landscape poetry and the ethnic diversity of Britain's Nobel literature laureates. It goes on to provide a more in-depth analysis, with close readings from an extraordinary scene in King Lear to a war poem by Carol Ann Duffy, and a series of striking examples of how literary texts change as they are transmitted from writer to reader.

{No reviews}

www.oup.com/vsi

ENVIRONMENTAL LAW

A Very Short Introduction

Elizabeth Fisher

Environmental law is the law concerned with environmental problems. It is a vast area of law that operates from the local to the global, involving a range of different legal and regulatory techniques. In theory, environmental protection is a no brainer. Few people would actively argue for pollution or environmental destruction. Ensuring a clean environment is ethically desirable, and also sensible from a purely self-interested perspective. Yet, in practice, environmental law is a messy and complex business fraught with conflict. Whilst environmental law is often characterized in overly simplistic terms, with a law being seen as be a simple solution to environmental problems, the reality is that creating and maintaining a body of laws to address and avoid problems is not easy, and involves legislators, courts, regulators, and communities.

This *Very Short Introduction* provides an overview of the main features of environmental law, and discusses how environmental law deals with multiple interests, socio-political conflicts, and the limits of knowledge about the environment. Showing how interdependent societies across the world have developed robust and legitimate bodies of law to address environmental problems, Elizabeth Fisher discusses some of the major issues and controversies involved in environmental law.

EUROPEAN UNION LAW
A Very Short Introduction
Anthony Arnull

The European Union is rarely out of the news and faces difficult questions about its future. In this debate, the law always has a central role to play.

In this *Very Short Introduction* Anthony Arnull looks at the laws and legal system of the European Union, including EU courts. He discusses the range of issues that the European Union has been given the power to regulate, such as the free movement of goods and people. Arnull considers why an organisation based on international treaties has proved capable of having far-reaching influence on both its Member States and on countries that lie beyond its borders.

www.oup.com/vsi

FREE SPEECH
A Very Short Introduction
Nigel Warburton

'I disapprove of what you say, but I will defend to the death your right to say it' This slogan, attributed to Voltaire, is frequently quoted by defenders of free speech. Yet it is rare to find anyone prepared to defend all expression in every circumstance, especially if the views expressed incite violence. So where do the limits lie? What is the real value of free speech? Here, Nigel Warburton offers a concise guide to important questions facing modern society about the value and limits of free speech: Where should a civilized society draw the line? Should we be free to offend other people's religion? Are there good grounds for censoring pornography? Has the Internet changed everything? This Very Short Introduction is a thought-provoking, accessible, and up-to-date examination of the liberal assumption that free speech is worth preserving at any cost.

> 'The genius of Nigel Warburton's *Free Speech* lies not only in its extraordinary clarity and incisiveness. Just as important is the way Warburton addresses freedom of speech - and attempts to stifle it - as an issue for the 21st century. More than ever, we need this book.'
>
> Denis Dutton, University of Canterbury, New Zealand

www.oup.com/vsi

GEOPOLITICS
A Very Short Introduction
Klaus Dodds

In certain places such as Iraq or Lebanon, moving a few feet either side of a territorial boundary can be a matter of life or death, dramatically highlighting the connections between place and politics. For a country's location and size as well as its sovereignty and resources all affect how the people that live there understand and interact with the wider world. Using wide-ranging examples, from historical maps to James Bond films and the rhetoric of political leaders like Churchill and George W. Bush, this Very Short Introduction shows why, for a full understanding of contemporary global politics, it is not just smart - it is essential - to be geopolitical.

'Engrossing study of a complex topic.'

Mick Herron, Geographical.

www.oup.com/vsi

GLOBALIZATION
A Very Short Introduction
Manfred Steger

'Globalization' has become one of the defining buzzwords of our time - a term that describes a variety of accelerating economic, political, cultural, ideological, and environmental processes that are rapidly altering our experience of the world. It is by its nature a dynamic topic - and this *Very Short Introduction* has been fully updated for 2009, to include developments in global politics, the impact of terrorism, and environmental issues. Presenting globalization in accessible language as a multifaceted process encompassing global, regional, and local aspects of social life, Manfred B. Steger looks at its causes and effects, examines whether it is a new phenomenon, and explores the question of whether, ultimately, globalization is a good or a bad thing.

www.oup.com/vsi

HUMAN RIGHTS
A Very Short Introduction
Andrew Clapham

An appeal to human rights in the face of injustice can be a heartfelt and morally justified demand for some, while for others it remains merely an empty slogan. Taking an international perspective and focusing on highly topical issues such as torture, arbitrary detention, privacy, health and discrimination, this *Very Short Introduction* will help readers to understand for themselves the controversies and complexities behind this vitally relevant issue. Looking at the philosophical justification for rights, the historical origins of human rights and how they are formed in law, Andrew Clapham explains what our human rights actually are, what they might be, and where the human rights movement is heading.

www.oup.com/vsi

INTERNATIONAL MIGRATION
A Very Short Introduction
Khalid Koser

Why has international migration become an issue of such intense public and political concern? How closely linked are migrants with terrorist organizations? What factors lie behind the dramatic increase in the number of women migrating? This *Very Short Introduction* examines the phenomenon of international human migration - both legal and illegal. Taking a global look at politics, economics, and globalization, the author presents the human side of topics such as asylum and refugees, human trafficking, migrant smuggling, development, and the international labour force.

www.oup.com/vsi

PHILOSOPHY OF LAW
A Very Short Introduction
SECOND EDITION
Raymond Wacks

The concept of law lies at the heart of our social and political life. Legal philosophy, or jurisprudence, explores the notion of law and its role in society, illuminating its meaning and its relation to the universal questions of justice, rights, and morality.

In this *Very Short Introduction* Raymond Wacks analyses the nature and purpose of the legal system, and the practice by courts, lawyers, and judges. Wacks reveals the intriguing and challenging nature of legal philosophy with clarity and enthusiasm, providing an enlightening guide to the central questions of legal theory.

In this revised edition Wacks makes a number of updates including new material on legal realism, changes to the approach to the analysis of law and legal theory, and updates to historical and anthropological jurisprudence.

THE UNITED NATIONS
A Very Short Introduction
Jussi M. Hanhimäki

With this much-needed introduction to the UN, Jussi Hanhimäki engages the current debate over the organization's effectiveness as he provides a clear understanding of how it was originally conceived, how it has come to its present form, and how it must confront new challenges in a rapidly changing world. After a brief history of the United Nations and its predecessor, the League of Nations, the author examines the UN's successes and failures as a guardian of international peace and security, as a promoter of human rights, as a protector of international law, and as an engineer of socio-economic development.

www.oup.com/vsi